June 1979

Congratulations

from

Mission Hills Baptist Church

After You Graduate

Decisions . . . . .
Changes . . . . .
Jobs . . . . .
College . . . . .

A Campus Life Book

After You Graduate

A guide to life after high school

Edited by
Steve Lawhead

Designed by
Joan Nickerson

ZONDERVAN PUBLISHING HOUSE
OF THE ZONDERVAN CORPORATION
GRAND RAPIDS, MICHIGAN 49506

CAMPUS LIFE BOOKS
A DIVISION OF YOUTH FOR CHRIST
WHEATON, ILLINOIS 60187

We are grateful to the publishers of the following for permission to reprint material appearing in this book: ⸺

"Is It True That I've Outgrown Her?" Excerpted from *Redbook* Magazine, May 1972, copyright © 1972, The Redbook Publishing Company.

"What If I Never Get Married?" Reprinted by permission from *HIS,* student magazine of InterVarsity Christian Fellowship, © 1973.

AFTER YOU GRADUATE
Copyright © 1978 by Youth for Christ International

Library of Congress Cataloging in Publication Data

After you graduate.

    1. High school seniors—Addresses, essays, lectures. 2. High school graduates—Employment—Addresses, essays, lectures. 3. College, Choice of—Addresses, essays, lectures. 4. College student orientation — Addresses, essays, lectures.

    I. Lawhead, Steve.

LB2350.A46   373.1'8   77-26649

Fourth printing April 1978

Padded: ISBN 0-310-36960-6
Paper: ISBN 0-310-36961-4

Printed in the United States of America

Contents

After You Graduate

Preface

Senioritis is an uncomfortable disease which strikes most people at least once in life: their senior year in high school. Diagnosis is simple. Ask casually, "By the way, what are you planning to do next year?"

In a mild case the eyes go slightly out of focus, and there is a long pause. A moderate case stutters and contradicts himself when he tries to answer. And a serious case lowers his or her head to the nearest table and blubbers helplessly.

Those with senioritis tend to huddle in little groups, nostalgically recalling all the wonderful things they did freshman year. They sigh a lot. No matter how they try to prevent it, their thoughts sneak past graduation into that great darkness optimistically called the future.

The problem is, How do you decide what's best to do? Your future rides on a decision about which you don't have enough information to make intelligently. No matter how many times you read the college catalogs, you don't know which school would really suit you.

You have no way of knowing which job you'll like (assuming you can get one at all). How can you know what you'll be like in two years?

If you're thinking about marriage, that throws an additional kink into any system you've worked out—nobody ever "reasoned" his way into marriage. That comes with heart thumping, nerves jangling and adrenalin flowing.

Christians seem to have the worst form of senioritis. They not only try to decide what *they* want to do, they try to get the opinion of a God whom they can't see or hear. They pray. They ask others to pray for them. They mumble things about God's will or spend time reading comforting psalms from the Bible. But often—too often—they have that same spark of fear in their eyes.

This book is for high school graduates (and anyone else who thinks he might be suffering from senioritis). It has been compiled mostly from articles which have appeared in CAMPUS LIFE Magazine. You'll find all sorts of information about your future—college, jobs, finding God's will, and a lot more. Enough to cure the worst case of senioritis.

Wallowitch

Decisions

Finding and securing God's approval for the future is a big part of a graduate's worries. You peer like a frustrated gypsy into a darkened crystal ball, trying to catch a glimpse of the shape of things to come. All you see are gigantic question marks.

This short section will help you in that search for answers. We put it first because after reading it many of your questions will shrink back into proper perspective. Some of our frustration with not being able to read the future centers, oddly enough, in our ever-persistent drive for happiness. We'll discuss that, too, and find out what place happiness has in deciding on our future.

John Chao

A happy future, bright with rosy opportunities and an all-lived-happily-ever-after ending is something everybody wants. So why don't more people succeed in finding the happiness they're after?

What Will Make Me Happy?

■ Happiness is not a very noble thing to want (not like wanting to be a great doctor). It's not exceptional, and certainly not particularly religious. However, I might as well admit it — with all my heart I want to be happy. It is practically the only thing I *do* want with "all my heart." It may also be the only desire I share with every single one of the four-billion-member human race.

Why happiness? There are plenty of other things human beings might want much more. We might want to help others. We might want to run the fastest mile ever. We might want to produce children. Any of those might be perfectly good as an end in itself — and far better that the "prize" of a temporary, satisfied grin. Yet we do them, generally, *only* if we think they will result in that grin, or that soft feeling inside which is our only criterion for judging whether we are in that blissful state called "happy."

Animals aren't particularly wrapped up in making themselves happy. They care about survival — once they find enough food and sufficient warmth, they go to sleep. Your dog, it's true, may spend a lot of time fetching sticks and wagging his tail at you, but in that case he's only caught the happiness disease from you. It is a rare dog who learns to fetch sticks by himself, alone in the wilds.

Of course, some animals do seem to be happy or sad. But even if they are, it's still something they only pursue in their spare time. We human beings, most of us, spend every waking hour plotting to catch that small elusive sensation. We're obsessed with it.

I am, anyway. I wake in the morning and, as I brush my hair, think about attracting a compliment or even a girl. The object? Happiness. I choose my breakfast cereal on the basis of which one tastes good, because good tastes make me happy. I play sports to win because I know how unhappy losing makes me feel. Ninety per cent of my efforts are motivated by my desire to be happy, whether in the short or the long term.

But why don't I succeed? I put all my efforts behind a search for happiness, and it seems relatively simple — a good bowl of ice cream, or a well-placed snowball can leave me smiling for hours. Yet there are whole days when *nothing* seems to work, and I feel miserable.

Vague Discomfort

Babies — very tiny babies — don't seem hung-up on happiness. They are

David S. Strickler

by Tim Stafford

motivated by pains in their stomach or wetness in their diapers. Once the discomfort is gone, they're quiet.

But that changes. Soon little children want more. They are not sure *what* they want: they can scream and rant after one thing, and then throw it away a few moments after they have it. They feel a void inside, and they try to fill it. They learn a whole list of techniques — throwing tantrums, showing off, being "good," being "cute." Some try to do well at school, in games, at drawing pictures or whatever seems likely to win love and make them happy.

Now, we are too grown up for that. Or are we? Most of us still behave like little children. We start working at removing our vague feelings of discomfort. Feel lonely? Make friends. Sometimes we cry or show off to get attention, but mostly we doggedly try to find the medicine to heal whatever hurts inside. Unfortunately, like children, we aren't sure just what *does* hurt. So, like a girl with so many toy horses they cover every inch of her room, it is always the *next* horse that will make us happy. Or if hundreds of horses have failed to satisfy, perhaps it is *boys*, or something else.

At one point in my life I thought it was

Decisions

awards I wanted: I won every award in sight, and had a big, top dresser drawer stuffed with certificates. Eventually I threw them out — they hadn't made me happy. Other times I thought if only I could learn to call up a girl and ask for a date without shaking I would be happy. Not so. At another point I thought having lots of friends and admirers was the key. By the time I had them I was wishing for more peace and quiet, and there was still an empty spot inside.

After many false starts, I think I've realized something: that I am not going to find happiness this way. Happiness, like a mirage, is always disappearing before me. I may as well give up the chase.

If you cling to your life, you will lose it, but if you give it up for me, you will save it (Matthew 10:39).

If anyone wants to be a follower of mine, let him deny himself and take up his cross and follow me (Matthew 16:24).

Unless a grain of wheat falls into the earth and dies, it remains itself alone, but if it dies, it bears much fruit. He who loves his life loses it, and he who hates his life in this world shall keep it to life eternal (John 12:24, 25).

Many men have noticed that *things* cannot make you happy. As far as I know, Jesus was the only man to suggest the final solution. "Die," he said. What did he mean?

I think he was speaking to me. I believe he was telling me, "Stop acting purely on your feelings." Rather than suggesting that I go on the long, painful task of re-vamping or extinguishing my desires, he suggested I short-circuit them: make a decision to follow him rather than them. The feelings are all right . . . they're human . . . but you can only follow one leader. When your feelings determine what you do, you're really following yourself. As I've seen it, I am not a very effective leader. That "leader" — myself — had to die.

Survival Tactics

Choosing to die to myself comes down to very practical, unmystical choices. For example: one friend of mine, Fred, could

Rohn Engh

"Happily ever after" is for fairy tales. Real happiness does not always lie in getting everything you want, your way.

get very concerned about girls — good-looking girls, that is. Then one day God seemed to be pointing him toward a girl who was fairly ugly. Taking her out was the last thing Fred wanted to do. But after struggling with his conscience for a while, he did it.

The girl didn't turn into a beautiful princess, nor did she introduce him to a beautiful girl Fred fell in love with. There was no "happy" outcome. The only happiness was that Fred had done what he should. He'd made a decision based on what God wanted, rather than on his feelings.

According to Jesus, these are "survival" tactics. They are not pleasure tactics. Jesus never said, "If you die for my sake, you'll go around with a big, happy smile on your face." The man who faced the cross despite his feelings knew better. He only said, "If you die for my sake, you will ultimately live."

Take money. What do you do with it? Do you look at it strictly in terms of how happy it will make you? Or do you want to find out what God wants, and trust your life to him?

Church: do you judge it by how happy it makes you feel, or by what you understand God wants you to do? Friends: do you choose those who make you feel good, or do you look for the ones God wants you to have?

Not that you're supposed to always choose the route of unhappiness. God's choice will often be — even usually be — the one you would normally want anyway. But he wants our good before our happiness — and there will be times when doing what is right will make you feel unhappy, at least temporarily.

But Christians are not unhappy people. It is a strange paradox that those who have turned away from following happiness often find their lives flooded with joy. They know happiness better, though they also seem to know how to cry better. Those who serve Jesus and their neighbors talk more about Jesus and their neighbors than about how happy they are. They are happy "by accident."

If there is a formula for happiness, it is this: forget it. Base your decisions on what is right, according to Jesus Christ. Stay close to him. In trying to do what you should, make up your mind to rejoice and be thankful, even in failure.

But be forewarned. The happiness God gives isn't the kind we imagine. Some people come to God as simply another road to happiness: after sex or drugs or prestige comes religion. But those motives have to change, because what they find will never be quite what they expected.

God's happiness is quite unlike what comes from being popular, or being elected to a high office, or living out sexual fantasies. In fact, those who experience God's happiness grow more and more indifferent to those things. God's happiness is a strange joy that can be thankful even when grief is heavy, one that can turn its back on pleasure when it has to. It is not a back door into the happiness you want so badly. It is the open front door to life and your future. ∎

By staying tuned in to what God wants, we will find the happiness we desire. That sounds easy, but there is one catch . . .

How Do I Know What God Wants

David S. Strickler

by Paul Little

■ If the Lord were to appear and grant you the answer to one question, what would you ask?

My guess is that it would probably relate to his will for your life. This is logical because our peace and satisfaction depend on knowing that God is guiding us.

But we are confused about what the will of God is. Most people speak of God's will as something you have or you don't have. Have you discovered God's will for your life?, someone may ask. In asking this question they usually mean, have you discovered God's *blueprint* for your life? The fact is that God seldom reveals an entire blueprint, and if you are looking for that blueprint, you are likely to be disappointed.

A sensational plus to being a Christian is knowing God has a plan. He has promised to reveal his will to us. "Trust in the Lord with all your heart, and do not rely on your own insight. In all your ways acknowledge him, and he will make straight your paths" (Proverbs 3:5, 6).

God's will has two sides. First, what he has revealed in the Bible. Second, the side where he has not set down specific guidelines.

Has it ever struck you that most of God's will has already been revealed in Scripture? These are the aspects of his will which apply to every Christian.

There are many positive commands. For instance, we are told by our Lord to go into all the world and preach the gospel to every creature. We know it is the will of God from Romans 8:29 to be conformed to the image of Christ. Read the book of James and make a list of all the commands that specifically apply to you.

Scripture contains many negative commands as well as positive ones. God tells us in unmistakable terms in 2 Corinthians 6:14 that we are not to be unequally yoked together with unbelievers. This means, among other things, that a Christian is never to marry an unbeliever. Are you praying for guidance about whether you should marry a non-Christian? Save your breath.

The late A. W. Tozer pointed out that we should never seek guidance about what God has already forbidden. Nor should we ever seek guidance in the areas where he has already said yes and given us a command. He then points out that in most things God has no preference. If you can choose your menu, he really does not have a great preference whether you have steak or chicken. He's not desperately concerned about whether you wear a green shirt or a blue shirt.

Then Tozer points out the second side of God's will, those areas where we need special guidance. In these areas of life

Decisions

there is no specific statement like "John Jones shalt be an engineer in Cincinnati," or "Thou, Mary Smith, shalt marry Fred Grotzenheimer." No verse in the Bible will give you that kind of detail in your life.

Dump the Blueprint Idea

By recognizing the two aspects of God's will — that which is already revealed in the Bible, and those areas about which he is not specific — you get away from the static concept of the blueprint. The will of God is not a package let down from heaven on a string.

It is far more like a scroll that unrolls every day. God has a will for you and me today, tomorrow and the next day and the day after that. Every one of us continues to seek the will of God throughout the whole of our lives.

Now it may well be that a decision you make will commit you for three months, or two years, or five or 10 years, or a lifetime. But the will of God is still something to be discerned and lived out every day. It is not something to be grasped once and for all.

Because of this, our call is not basically to a plan, a blueprint, a place or a work, but our call is basically to follow the Lord Jesus Christ.

What are the prerequisites for knowing the will of God? The first is *to be a child of God*. One day some people asked Jesus directly, "What must we do to be doing the works of God?" And Jesus answered, "This is the work of God, that you believe in him whom he has sent" (John 6:29).

We must first come to the Lord Jesus Christ in a commitment of faith to him as Savior and Lord. Then we are God's children and can be guided by him as our Father.

A second prerequisite: *we need to be obeying God where we know his will.* What's the point of God guiding us in areas where he's not been specific when we're apparently unconcerned about areas where he is specific?

The third prerequisite: *we must be willing to accept the will of God*, without knowing what it is. We need to accept it in advance, in other words. For most of us, I suspect, this is where the real problem lies. If we're honest, most of us would have to admit that our attitude is, "Lord, show me what your will is so I can decide whether it fits in with what I have in mind and whether I want to do it or not. Lord, show me whether I'm to be married or not. Show me where in the world you want me to go and what you want me to do so I can decide. If it's Palm Beach or Honolulu, or some wonderful place like that, maybe then I'll consider it a little more seriously."

That attitude reflects the fact that we do not trust God to know best what will work out for our lives. We don't believe he has our good at heart. We're saying, "I think I know better, God, what will make me happy, and I'm afraid to trust my life to you; you're going to shortchange me." Have you ever felt that? It's a solemn thing to realize. We make the tragic mistake of thinking that the choice is between doing what we want to do and being happy, and doing what God wants us to do and being miserable. We think the will of God is some terrible thing he shoves under our nose and says, "Are you willing, are you willing?" We think that if we could just get out from under his clammy hands we could really hang loose.

God Is No Scrooge

We see God as a celestial Scrooge who leans down over the balcony of heaven trying to find anybody who's enjoying life, and says "Now cut it out." But we

If we're honest, most of us would have to admit that our attitude is, "Lord, show me what your will is so I can decide whether I want to do it or not "

need to have the tremendous truth of Romans 8:32 deeply planted in our hearts: "He who did not spare his own Son but gave him up for us all, will he not also give us all things with him?" If you can get hold of that verse and allow it to

get hold of you, you will have solved 90 per cent of your problem about desiring the will of God.

You'll realize that the God who loved you and me enough to die for us when we didn't care about him is not about to shortchange us when we give our lives to him. As Oswald Hoffman of the Lutheran Hour has put it, having given us the package, do you think God will deny us the ribbon? What nonsense.

I have two children, a daughter Debbie, and a son Paul. My children come to me and say, "Daddy, I love you" Do I respond by saying, "Ah, children, that's just what I've been waiting to hear. Into the closet for three weeks. Bread and water. I've just been waiting for you to tell me you love me so I can make your life miserable." Do you think that's the way I respond?

They can get anything they want out of me at that point!

Do you think God is any less loving than a human father? God's love so far transcends any love we humans have that it can never be expressed. The Lord is constantly drawing contrasts between human love and our heavenly Father's love. If you, being evil, he says in Luke 11:15, know how to give good gifts to your children, how much more shall your heavenly Father give the Holy Spirit when you ask him.

When we come to God and say, "I love you and I'm prepared to do your will, whatever you want me to do," we can be sure that God rejoices and fits our lives into his pattern for us, that place where he in his omniscience and love knows we will fit hand and glove. He is our Creator, and knows us better that we will ever know ourselves.

God's will is not loathsome. It's the greatest thing in all of life to get hold of. There's no greater joy or satisfaction than to be in the center of God's will and know it. In his autobiography, *Shadow of the Almighty*, Jim Elliot (later martyred by Auca Indians) spoke of the "sheer joy" of doing the will of God.

How Does God Guide?

First, through principles. Take, for instance, the statement in Psalm 15:4 that God is pleased with a person who swears to his own hurt and does not repent. What this means is that our word is as good as our bond; we don't break commitments or contracts without being released. We assume responsibility and live up to it, a feature very lacking in much of our society today.

I remember several years ago a person who in August got an offer of a job, which was closer to where she wanted to live, and broke a contract to teach at a particular school. The department chairman who told me about this Christian girl's action said her justification was, "I have peace about it," and he commented rather sardonically, "Isn't that wonderful that she has the peace and I have the pieces?" I believe that girl missed the will of God, because she violated a principle, which would have given very clear guidance in a specific detail of life. God guides us

through his Word and its principles.

Second, he guides us in prayer as we ask him to show us his will. I can remember Dr. T. Norton Sterrett who asked, "How many of you who are concerned about the will of God spend even five minutes a day asking him to show you his will?" It was like someone had grabbed me around the throat. I was rushing around going to this meeting, reading that book, trying this little formula to discover the will of God. I was doing everything but getting in the presence of God and asking him to show me what his will for me was.

Through prayer he often gives us a conviction by the Holy Spirit that deepens despite new information. This is quite different from the emotion which causes us to be interested in this today and that tomorrow and something else the day after tomorrow.

Third, he guides through circumstances. Here, however, we must be particularly on guard. Most of us make circumstances 99% of the guidance. We must view them with God's perspectives and values.

Circumstances may be more of a guide negatively than positively. For instance, if you think God is leading you to college and you can't get into any school in this country or abroad, it may be fairly clearcut evidence that God wants you to do something else. On the other hand, the fact that you got into three medical schools doesn't necessarily mean God wants you to go into medicine. There may be other factors to consider.

Just because you have a job opening in

this country doesn't mean you should stay here. Familiarize yourself with the needs of the world. Ninety per cent of the Christian workers are in parts of the world that have 10% of the world's population, and 10% of the full-time Christian workers are in population centers having 90% of the world's population.

It may well be that we should make every effort to go overseas unless God clearly calls us to stay home rather than the reverse. He can close doors very easily. But he can't steer us in the right directions if we're not moving.

Fourth, God guides us through the counsel of other Christians who are equally committed to the will of God and who know us well. I believe personally that this is one of the most neglected dimensions of guidance in the lives of many Christians. It sounds terribly spiritual for a person to say "God led me," but I am always suspicious of the person who seems to imply he has a private pipeline to God when no one else senses this is God's will. God has been blamed for the most outlandish things by people who have confused their own inverted spiritual pride with his will.

A guy occasionally in the name of guidance will walk up to a girl and say, "Susie, God has led me to marry you." Well, I have news for Joe: if it's God's will that Susie is to marry him, Susie will get the message, too, and if she doesn't, somebody's radar is jammed.

Are you wondering about marriage? Do you wonder what your gifts are? Talk to some of your mature Christian friends,

God guides in many ways, but he never hijacks our minds or forces us to become robots for his plans.

Bob Combs

Decisions

your pastor and others who know you and are concerned for the will of God themselves. Don't be afraid to talk to people whom you think may give you advice you don't want to hear. It may be you are emotionally involved in a particular situation and you can't see it objectively. You need someone to talk really straight so you can be realistic.

Roadblocks to Avoid

In considering God's will, there are some serious mistakes to avoid.

(1) We must not think that because we *want* to do something it cannot possibly be God's will. God isn't a killjoy. We need to realize the wonderful truth of Psalm 37:4 where David says, "Delight thyself also in the Lord, and he shall give thee the desires of thine heart."

This doesn't mean that if we delight ourselves in the Lord, he will give us anything we want. What it means is that as we delight in the Lord we come, as the hymn says, to will with him one will. And the greatest joy of all our lives is to do what the Lord wants us to do.

(2) We must guard against the idea that every decision we make must have a subjective confirmation. If you are facing a big decision about which God has not given you specific guidance, wait on it. If you need to decide immediately, do so. God does not play mousetrap with us and say, "Ah ha, you thought you were down the right lane, but you were wrong. Go back to the start and try again." We can trust him. Proverbs 3:5, 6: "Trust in the Lord with all your heart, lean not unto your own understanding, in all your ways acknowledge him, and he shall direct your paths."

(3) We must not necessarily think God's will is wild and bizarre. It may well be that he will lead us to do something that is contrary to unenlightened reason,

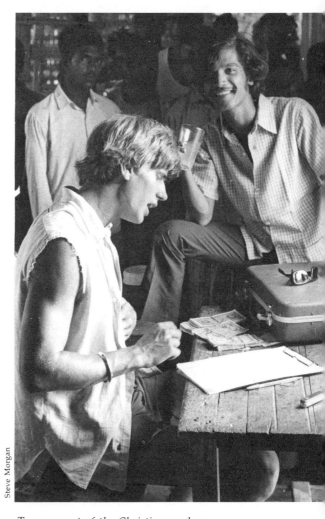

Steve Morgan

Ten per cent of the Christian workers serve 90% of the world's population — maybe God wants you to join that neglected 10%.

but that his will is frequently bizarre is a dangerous assumption. Some people seem to feel that unless a thing is totally outlandish it couldn't be the will of God.

(4) We must guard against the subtle temptation to decide what we are going to do for God. There is a vast difference between saying "Lord, I'm going to be a businessman for you," or "Lord, I'm going to be a missionary for you," and saying "Lord, what will you have me to do?"

(5) We must guard against the temptation of taking verses out of context to get God's will. Some people seem to think the Bible is a magic book. You can't flip through it, place your finger on a verse with your eyes closed and expect that God will speak to your specific need in that verse. Because of this violation of a basic Biblical principle in interpreting and understanding the Bible, God has been blamed for all kinds of things which were merely human stupidity.

(6) We must avoid the mistake of thinking we are in the will of God because everything is going smoothly. Frequently, it is when we have taken a step of obedience that the bottom falls out of everything. Then, it is only the confidence that we are in the will of God that keeps us going. The test of whether or not you are in the will of God is not how rosy your circumstances are, but whether you are *obeying* him.

(7) It is also crucial to avoid the mistake of thinking that a call to world evangelism or missionary service is any different from a call to anything else. Dr. T. N. Sterrett, in his helpful booklet "Called by God and Sure of It," points out that every Christian has both the privilege and the responsibility to know whether he should serve in Cairo or Chicago. The crucial question each of us must ask ourselves is, "Am I in the will of God and sure of it?"

(8) We must avoid the mistake of thinking that if we have ever knowingly and deliberately disobeyed the Lord we are forever thrown on the ash heap, can never do his will and are doomed to second best. God in a very wonderful way has ways of reweaving the strands of our lives and taking us where we are, as we come to him in confession and repentance, and using us fully. Our disobedience did not take him by surprise, and his grace reaches to us.

God's will for you? Realize first that God's will in most of its aspects is already fully revealed, and be sure you are familiar with it. In those areas about which he is not specific, be assured he will guide you through the Bible and its principles as you seek his face in prayer and as you view the circumstances from his point of view and seek the counsel of other Christians. As you come to the place of saying, "Lord, I want to do your will more than anything else in life," and as you avoid some of the mistakes based very often on a distortion of the character of God, you will know where in the world and how in the world he wants you to serve him. ∎

Based on a talk given by the late Paul Little at the Urbana Missionary Conference, syndicated by the Evangelical Press Association.

Changes

Now that you're finally out of high school all the things you've been waiting for will start happening. Some things in your life will change immediately — no more tardy passes, assigned lockers or study halls. Other things will change more gradually. You'll begin growing away from those closest to you — your parents. You'll be exposed to a larger world than you knew existed. What's more, you'll be on your own to a greater extent than before.

The biggest changes will be relationships. Your circle of friends will grow wider. You'll meet new friends as old friendships fade. You'll begin dating more. (It might surprise you, but most people don't date very much in high school. After graduation that changes.)

Those changes and the adjustments you'll have to make are the subjects of this next section.

Soon you'll begin seeing your parents in a different light.
The next two stories show how two people adjusted to
a new distance from their parents.

Is It True That I've Outgrown Her?

■ By the time I was 16, I was three inches taller than my mother. My mother and I had a joke between us during that time. Since daughters usually end up taller than their mothers, we reasoned with mock seriousness, mothers must surely shrink.

During my freshman year at college I began to wonder if my mother hadn't shrunk mentally as well. By the time I came home for the holidays I realized that not only could I reach kitchen shelves Mother couldn't touch but my mind, too, was exploring heights toward which she'd never stretched.

Over the next three years of school I became unhappily aware of a wider and wider gap between us. We couldn't agree on religion, books, current political issues, academic freedom or what goals one should aim for in life. Our polite talks often exploded into hot arguments.

When I thought of mother's sacrifices that let me get where I was, I'd nearly weep. I had turned into the kind of daughter I thought I'd never be — one whose seeming ingratitude was breaking her parents' hearts. I finally vowed to bite my tongue until it bled rather than argue with Mom again.

All went well for three years and several short visits. Mom and I had never

Wallowitch

by Ann R. Eddy

discussed the no-argument plan, but it was as though we both knew the rules perfectly. Most old subjects were taboo, and new, potentially explosive subjects were avoided with care. Unfortunately, we were acting more like polite acquaintances than mother and daughter, and our relationship was becoming shallow and sad.

In the fourth year of our delicate truce my husband was to present a paper at the medical convention in mid-August, and this seemed a good time for me to spend a few days with Mom and Dad. Within an hour of my arrival Mother and I had exchanged all the "safe" news — as usual. Three days of small talk loomed ahead.

Two of my mother's friends came for lunch that first day. I hadn't seen them in years, and so for a while I enjoyed their light chatter. But four hours of talk about grandchildren, the weather and African violets exhausted me. I was annoyed, too, when they assumed that their rather slick, neat views on an occasional, more complex subject would naturally be mine as well.

When Mother finally had closed the front door on her departing guests she said to me, "Honey, you didn't have much to say. I do wish you had talked a little more."

"Mother," I burst out, "I didn't talk because I was bored! Don't you see that you and I have nothing in common? You either don't approve of or you don't understand everything I find worthwhile!"

I was shocked to hear my dark anger pour out into the light. My knees turned to jelly and I sank into a handy chair. Mother sat down more slowly, as if she were bravely sustaining an arrow through her heart.

But when she spoke it was as if she had read my old thoughts. "You've outgrown me, Ann," she said evenly. "It's hard for a mother to accept, but you have, and I think it always happens. I outgrew my mother. When I was your age I'd go back home to the farm and think I was going to scream from boredom. No one ever talked about anything but the crops; no one ever asked anything but 'How are your hens laying?'

"And once, in a very regrettable moment, I told my mother that she and Papa were dull and old-fashioned. Mama sat down with tears tracing the deep wrinkles of her cheeks and said, 'But, Nancy, that's because you've outgrown us. Papa and I raised you with the hope that you'd do things and learn things we've never had the chance to do or learn. Our sacrifices have nurtured the very growth that's made you find us dull.' And then Mama said slowly, but with a strange pride, 'I reckon your feelings are proof of our success.' "

This was one of those crystal moments in life when you see yourself as part of an endless chain. This time it was a chain of mothers and daughters winding back through untold generations, every child outgrowing her mother by a little or a lot, only to make sacrifices for her own child and be outgrown herself.

Perhaps Mother and I saw the same chain, because the old chasm between us miraculously filled. For the first time in years we stood on solid, communicable ground. Our first exchange, I must say, wasn't very articulate. I found myself with my arms around my mother as we gave soggy comfort through our tears. In the days that followed, the easy warmth of those moments held fast.

Slowly we began to tackle those points of disagreement that had separated us over the past several years. Now the air was clear. The urgency was gone. We were willing to compromise, to admit agreement when we saw it, to acknowledge a good point on the other side and, most of all, to listen.

We ended up still disagreeing about quite a few things. But our eager, open talks had shown me a wisdom in my mother I'd never known before — or maybe I'd just forgotten it.

By the next summer my dear mother had died. We had parted in love and respect. I knew I was what I was because of her. And I knew she had known that. ■

■ I was full of excitement as I stuffed my Datsun with suitcases, typewriter and books. From a small town in the Pennsylvania mountains I'd travel to Chicago. New challenges. New friends.

My parents shared my enthusiasm. Together, we had a commitment to Christ. We respected and loved each other. I'd miss them.

But my brain was on Chicago, and my emotions flowed toward the future. I was intent on new worlds.

They sent letters several times a week. At Christmas and Easter they welcomed

What Is It Like To Let Go?

me like I'd come home from East Asia.

But what did they really feel?

I got a hint not long after I left them. I met Jeanette in Wisconsin and took her to Pennsylvania at Christmas. I put the ring on her finger and we walked into the kitchen and made our announcement.

Amid all the congratulations and smiles and joy sneaked in the words, "Well, Harold, you didn't get your girl from Pennsylvania, did you?" It was meant to be humorous, a side remark, filler. But it came up out of a deep yearning. A Wisconsin girl meant less chance I'd live nearby. Why'd they have to think about that?

Only one way would I understand: later, Jeanette and I had a baby girl, Michelle. And now a little boy, Todd.

How can I describe my emotions toward them? Holding them. Talking to them. Throwing them into the air. If any-

by Harold Myra

Betty Outlaw

thing happened to them, it would slice deep. I loved them like . . . like I loved Jeanette.

And I guess that's the parallel.

I used to dream of finding *the* girl. Building a life together. Enjoying each other. Planning together for a lifetime. I always knew that, once in love, breaking apart would be like sawing me in half.

And now, it's the same with Michelle and Todd. Until I was a dad myself, I never dreamed my love for them would be as strong as my love for Jeanette. Or that breaking from them would be as tough in some ways as seeing Jeanette walk away from me.

Oh, I don't intend to become a clinging parent. Mine weren't. But as Todd and Michelle grow toward all the excitement of their futures — they won't feel what I will: this oneness with them. They'll be all wrapped up in college or engagements or career.

So, I'm psyching myself to enjoy feeling them a little at a time. Then to enjoy watching them fly from the nest with strong wings. Sure I'll smile and laugh and share their enthusiasm as they leave. But I don't expect them to look back and understand my feelings. I didn't a few years ago. I had to get this bond with Michelle and Todd to understand what my parents felt the day I packed that Datsun. Their tears mixed with their hugs and handshakes meant more than a warm ritual — it was a ripping of fabric, like birth ripping through the living tissue of the mother.

It's natural — the mixture of pain and joy. But somehow I wish I'd understood all that the day I hugged Mom and Dad good-bye. ■

Your love life is about to take an active up-swing. That tight
little group you hung around with in high school will expand rapidly
after graduation. You'll come into contact with many more
Christians and non-Christians you'll want to date.
Then you'll wonder (if you haven't already) . . .

_____ What About Dating No

Bob Combs

hristians?   by Steve Lawhead

■"I am now 18 and have been dating a non-Christian since last August. She respects my commitment to God, as well as my morals, but she doesn't share my beliefs. Our relationship has grown from a casual friendship into a deep love for each other. Now, as I consider the future, I realize what a step I was taking in deciding to date her. I can't marry her, for our relationship wouldn't be a Christian union dedicated to God. Yet, I am very serious about her. The result is one frustrated guy, struggling with his emotions. I constantly pray for her to come to Christ, but the longer I wait, the less I want to give her up. I am afraid that I may someday choose to marry her despite the situation. I can only hope and pray that the day will never come."

Alex

"I'm a Christian girl who is dating a non-Christian guy. I have to admit I love him, although people tell me that now, as a Christian, I have to drop him. I can't. That's my problem.

I witness to him, but I try not to offend him by preaching at him. I don't expect him to accept my new life right away, but I just can't say, 'I don't think God approves of us dating because I'm a Christian and you're not.' He'd really hate God, and what good is that? I feel that once I've opened his eyes we can go on, and through me he can eventually see God. What do you think?"

Debbie

"I just started dating a guy who is not a Christian. I am a Christian, and so far religion hasn't come up. I would never let him change the way I think — although I'd like to change him. I don't think anything serious will arise in our relationship, but do you think it is wrong to continue dating him?"

Karen

These letters, like scores of others, represent people who have one thing in common — a problem in their love life. The names and places change, but basically the problem is the same. They want an answer: is it all right, or not all right?

But what's all the fuss? Dating's just for fun — a good way to meet people. What does religion have to do with it anyway? The Bible says a Christian shouldn't marry a non-Christian, but it doesn't say anything about not dating them, so why not? As long as you behave yourself and everyone has a good time, what's the problem?

Usually there isn't any — at first. The relationship goes along just fine until something happens: the person you started out dating "just for fun" suddenly becomes someone special. And if you are a Christian and the special someone isn't, sooner or later, you've got a problem. What do you do? You can either write a letter to "Dear Abby" for help, or think it through, following a few basic guidelines.

Christians and non-Christians don't appear terribly different. But while they may look, act and feel the same, even share the same moral outlook, they're miles apart. Christians believe in an all-important relationship with Christ as the foundation for everything. Non-Christians (by definition) do not.

Trouble Up Ahead

Trouble starts when a Christian wants so badly to continue a deepening relationship with a non-Christian that he'd give up Christ — something no Christian consciously, rationally wants to do. But in affairs of the heart, conscience often takes a back seat. As the romance develops, you begin to see the classic picture of a Christian twisting and squirming, trying to avoid making a most painful decision: whether to give up Jesus or the loved one, or to try to live somewhere in between the two. (This is the point where most people write letters.)

Just because a person is dating a non-Christian doesn't mean he has to give up his Christianity, does it? No, not at all, but you should know the risks involved in beginning a relationship with a non-Christian. Really there's only one risk: that you'll fall in love.

If you could ever be sure that you wouldn't, it would solve half your worries. But anytime you enter a relationship with a member of the opposite sex, you open the door for all kinds of funny things to happen. So much depends upon your view of dating, your maturity and how firm your faith is, it's hard to say what might happen.

Truthfully, most people don't think about whether the person they are asking out next Saturday night is a Christian, or even consider it something they *ought* to think about. Julie Lattier, a bright, perky 17-year-old high-school senior, is somewhat unusual because she does.

"I went out with one boy who wasn't a Christian a couple of times. After the second date, I had seen enough to know that our attitudes were so completely different, there was no way I could continue seeing him unless a change was made. The things that were important to me — the church, prayer, my relationship with Jesus — he laughed at.

"So, as he drove me home that night I tried to explain to him that I felt we were too far apart in our beliefs for us to continue seeing each other. I liked him as a person, and he liked me, but his lack of respect for my feelings made a deeper relationship impossible. He understood because he knew I was a Christian from the start, but he persisted in trying to get me to give in.

"We sat in his car out in front of my house for the longest time talking about it. He said, 'I think it would be okay if you believe what you believe, and I believe what I believe. Then we could get along.' I didn't want to be unreasonable, so I asked him, 'What do you believe in?' He thought for a moment and then stuttered a bit and fell silent. He couldn't think of one thing he really believed in.

"We sat quiet for a minute and finally I said, 'If we were to continue seeing each other on a romantic level, eventually I would have to make a choice between Christ and you. You know who'd win?' He looked at me kind of funny, like I was crazy. 'Who?' he said, as if there was any doubt in his mind. I really think he didn't realize Jesus would always have first place with me."

A Little Respect

Julie's example brings up several of the most important guidelines to follow when beginning a relationship with a non-Christian. First of all, she knew herself and she knew her faith. She was secure enough in her relationship with Christ not to let anything interfere with it. As nice as a date with a boy could be, dating *someone* was not so important to her as dating someone who respected her beliefs and feelings.

Also, Julie was willing to break off a relationship with a non-Christian when she realized there could be no future in it. Rather than lead him on or try to change him, she let him go, which is what a Christian must always be prepared to do. Her faith was not directly threatened. She was not faced with a choice between her friend and Jesus right then and there, but she knew eventually, if the relationship were to grow romantically, a choice like

Truthfully, most people don't think about whether the person they are asking out next Saturday night is a Christian, or even consider it something they ought to think about

that would have to be made.

Many times Christians kid themselves into thinking their non-Christian friend *needs* them to show him the way. It sometimes happens that way — a non-Christian will come to the Lord as a result of the Christian influence of a boyfriend or girl friend. More often, however, it works the other way around. Trying to convert someone you are deeply, emotionally attached to usually causes more problems than it solves; furthermore, you can't always be sure your interest in his conversion isn't merely a selfish desire on your

Changes

part, designed to keep you from feeling guilty about enjoying yourself with him.

Another important aspect of any relationship is communication. "I've noticed in my experience dating non-Christians that I can't really communicate at the deepest level with them," Julie says. "There are certain things, basic things, I can't talk about, such as the power of the Lord in my life, something I learned from a Bible study or my spiritual struggles. I

Trying to convert someone you are deeply, emotionally attached to usually causes more problems than it solves

find myself avoiding subjects that are important to me because they either turn the guy off, or he just doesn't understand." Certainly, that kind of communication is not important in all relationships, but a long-term, growing relationship cannot exist without it.

Is It Wrong?

All this is not to say it's always wrong to date a non-Christian. It isn't. But it seems a little short of miraculous the way so many Christians suddenly "find" themselves deeply entangled in a romantic relationship with a non-Christian, being pulled in two directions at once,

crying for help. A situation like that is serious, but it needn't happen — not if you keep your eyes open and remember three simple guidelines.

1) A Christian must maintain his own priorities and standards, having them firmly in place *before* accepting a date. Know your standards of behavior, your sexual limits and even where you will go and what you will do on a date.

2) You must always know where you stand with Christ. Relationships change, and a Christian must constantly evaluate himself and his friends in light of his Christian principles.

3) A Christian must always be willing to break off a relationship with a non-Christian. Some people aren't secure enough in themselves and in their faith to handle that situation. For them, it's probably best they don't date non-Christians at all. *Know yourself.* Some people save a lot of heartaches by simply never dating non-Christians; if you're susceptible to falling in love, it's a good rule.

However, even avoiding dating non-Christians isn't easy when you realize that statistically there are more Christian girls than guys. With fewer Christian guys to go around, it works out that a girl could stay home quite a bit.

There are no easy answers, but having your own head straight, spiritual priorities in order and standards set is the fairest and easiest way to begin any relationship — particularly when it involves a member of the opposite sex. That's really only common sense, and that's what takes the worry out of being close. ■

When you find someone you'd like to get to know a whole lot better, most likely sex will enter the picture, too. Pressures to have sex are incredible today. The reasons to hold off don't seem able to stand up any more. Besides, when you get down to it . . .

What Difference Does a Piece of

Richard T. Lee

Paper Make? by Tim Stafford

■ Today's new sexual attitudes have raised all the old questions again. You know them.

What's wrong with sex, *if we really love each other?*

If we're going to get married anyway?

If sex is really supposed to be beautiful?

I've had to think about those questions a lot. I've spent four years in coed college dorms. I know what it's like to come home wondering whether it's safe to interrupt your roommate and his girl friend. I've seen the movies and read the books. I've argued in lots of bull sessions. I've spent hours trying to convince close friends they ought to wait for marriage.

So I know how the arguments go. I've had mine battered down by the insistent, *Why not?*

I know how the feelings go, too. You feel like a child when you argue for virginity. Everyone, you think, is smirking at you and saying, "What does he know? He's a virgin himself."

Nearly all the Christian books argue things like, *You'll feel terrible guilt later.* Or, *you face the threat of unwanted children, the threat of a venereal disease.* Or, *men really want to marry pure women.* They're actually good arguments, especially when you read statistics and find out that only 25 per cent of our sexually-liberated teenagers use any birth control devices regularly. Or when you read about the spread of VD. Or when you find out that, for all the signs of liberation, people (and especially girls) often *do* feel guilty about their sex life.

But those arguments don't convince most people. For one thing, irrational as it may be, guilt and VD and pregnancy are things that only happen to "other people." More important, they're all answerable by those "what-if" arguments. "What if" we use birth control?

The other side was what I saw gradually happen to my free-sex friends. No, they aren't lying in asylums tearing out their hair over a nameless, all-pervading guilt. Nothing so spectacular as that. In fact, nothing spectacular at all. That's just it. Sex seems to either become a compulsion that takes all their mental energy and yet leaves them unhappy, or it becomes just ho-hum. Mostly the latter. They simply don't act like the excited, happy, fulfilled people free sex advertised it would make them. In fact, quite a few of them are in their twenties now, still on the loose, lonely and a little less proud of being liberated. Some have been married and divorced a time or two.

So I've held onto the Christian side. My Christian friends, married or unmarried, didn't seem damaged by the "mindless repression" of waiting for marriage. They seemed, in fact, almost smugly happy.

The Moral Minority

And there was another argument that was convincing to me, though hardly for my non-Christian friends. It goes, "The Bible says."

I'd discovered that the Bible had a much higher batting average than I did for finding the right way to live.

But my non-Christian friends weren't having any of that. "Don't give me that authoritarian stuff," they'd say. "If it makes sense, it has to make sense to me, right now!"

I'd guess that speech is going to get stronger in the next five years. It's already strong enough. About half the unmarried girls who reach 20 are no longer virgins. It's more with the guys: maybe 70-90%, depending on whose survey you believe. In this kind of atmosphere the Hugh Hefners will stop saying, "Here's why your version of morality is dated." It's going to be the Christians saying to the Hugh Hefners, "Here's why *your* version of morality is dated." Christians have always been in the minority: now our morals are, too.

I'm not going to raise all those guilt arguments a lot of Christians raise, nor am I going to talk about VD or pregnancy. I won't question whether your motives for wanting premarital sex are pure. I won't doubt that you're really in love, and that you left puppy love behind years ago. I won't even question your level of

unselfish commitment to each other. Those are important questions in regard to premarital sex. But you can throw the "what-if" arguments at them — so I'll skip them.

I ask you to make only one assumption. I want to assume you are after the greatest sex possible. No substitutes accepted. You want the gourmet stuff, the stuff only a few people ever achieve in this hung-up world. You want a whole lifetime of it. None of this stuff about, "Well, I had a great thing going with this chick (or guy) for a couple of years, and I've been trying to find something like that ever since." You want a whole lifetime of great, loving sex in a terrific relationship with another person.

Maybe you say, "Sure! Of course that's what I want." But think about it. Don't tell me that there isn't lots of animalistic selfishness in your sexual appetite. I know all about that. I've been noticing it in myself for quite a few years now, and you aren't that different.

There's a lot of sexploitation going on. Some people would even claim it's the best philosophy: "Get all you can when you can." "Love 'em and leave 'em." A subtler, modern version is, "You should stay together as long as you're in love, but when you're not in love anymore, why endure the pain?" (Translated: when you get tired of your lover, let your emotions rule. Drop the has-been!)

But leave those arguments. Right now let's talk about the very finest sex: sex in a giving, growing, fulfilled relationship; sex in marriage as marriage was meant to be. The question is, "What difference does a piece of paper make?"

What does a Christian say? What difference *does* a piece of paper make?

That's what Chuck wanted to know. He's one of the kindest, gentlest people I've ever met. He met Elaine at the end of our freshman year. She was going to graduate, and they might not see each other for a long time. It just seemed so right, so natural for them to sleep together. It was a fulfillment of the love they

Breaking up is painful enough anyway, but sex makes it worse

felt for each other. And they really were in love. It was going to last.

So that summer Chuck worked on road construction, and all he could think about was Elaine. Finally he decided: he couldn't stand waiting any longer, so he quit his job and hitched about 2,000 miles to her hometown. It was a long, lonely trip, and he got there really tired. But he was happy.

Until he saw Elaine. She had met another guy, and Chuck didn't fit into the picture anymore. So Chuck hitched all the way back, starting the next day, and there was a sadness and a sickness in his gut like you wouldn't believe.

FACT #1: *Love that comes on like lightning may leave just as quickly.*

You may think you have the greatest thing going since Romeo and Juliet, and maybe you do. But maybe you don't. Kick yourself off the pedestal. Don't believe the "We're different" speech. You know perfectly well that there are millions of loves that "really were going to last" but didn't. You're no different from the rest of the world. Your interests change. Your moods change. You'll be a different person a month from now. You'll be even more different five years from now. And a girl or a guy who infatuated you one day doesn't the next.

FACT #2: *Sex makes it a lot harder on you when you split up.*

Breaking up is painful enough anyway, but sex makes it worse. Sex isn't like food, which you can push away when you're not hungry and forget all about. Sex takes in everything: it's meant to express a total commitment. Even when you cheat and try to use it with less than a total, lifetime commitment, there's often a kickback. It won't lie down and play dead. It binds you to the person spiritually, mentally, emotionally. And when the time comes for breaking up, it tears. Walter Trobisch says this is like trying to separate two pieces of paper that have been glued together. You can't do it without tearing one or the other. People know this inside, no matter how liberated they talk: people who make love weren't made to be torn apart.

Of course, if you let yourself be torn this way enough times, it stops hurting. But do you want to let yourself be that callous?

Changes

But I can hear the murmurs. "This is different. We're *going* to get married. In fact, we consider ourselves married. We're not going to split up."

FACT #3: *Premarital sex doesn't help you stay together. It'll help pull you apart.*

Let me tell you about Gail. Her family was quiet and conservative, and so was she. She seldom said a word, and when she did it was so soft you usually had to ask her to repeat it. But she was beautiful: long, blonde hair; sleepy, blue eyes; perfect skin. She met Peter, and to everyone's surprise they started sleeping together, then living together. Pete told me, "I've finally found her. I think this is it . . . for life."

It's been three years, and they are still living together. But living together is about all they're doing. They seldom talk; they don't have mutual friends. And sometimes Pete tells his friends he is tired of it. He would like to take off. Gail is a burden on him.

Gail has grown up a little, too. She has a mind of her own now. Lately she has been wondering if Peter is really right for her. Once last year she went on a trip and was gone for five weeks. She never wrote him: what did they have to say? She did come back: showed up one day and didn't say a word to indicate she'd been gone. Will she come back next time? None of their friends would bet on it. And actually, most of the friends don't care.

Frustration Kills?

Some of those really liberated people will tell you that not indulging in sex will break up your relationship. They say the frustration will kill you, that it's not natural.

Don't believe them. A little frustration is good for you. For one thing, it's a testing point: are you willing to live with a little pain? Do you care about each other enough as people not to worry about giving something up? If your friendship can't take a little frustration, you'd better forget it.

But there's an even more important point. A little frustration will draw you together if your love is for real. Satisfying it outside of a marriage commitment can push you apart.

You see one reason operating between Gail and Peter. When you're sleeping together, you have the illusion you're as together as you can be. Sex is meant, after all, to be the ultimate in expression. It certainly feels like it.

But the feelings can be phony. You can feel you're expressing your heart and soul when all you're expressing is your horniness. And when sex is phony like that, it never gets very deep. The first time it may be tremendous. Even if it isn't tremendous, at least it's the first time. That in itself is exciting.

But the twentieth time it may be old hat. Oh, you'll never get tired of the sex act itself: not unless you're weird. But you might get tired of the same partner. If it's mostly a physical pleasure it really doesn't matter *who* you do it with. And this is when people like Peter and Gail, who never learned to love each other very deeply as persons in the first place or made deep, permanent commitments, eventually drift apart. What might have been beautiful turns out to be a drag — because they wouldn't put up with a little frustration while they took time to get to know each other.

Something has to pull you together while you get to know each other. It takes time. Not just time kissing or snuggling — time talking about every blessed subject under the sun, time doing things together and going all kinds of places. And

Philip Yancey

A little sexual frustration will actually draw you closer together as you look for new ways to express your love.

what is that something that pulls you together? A lot of it is sexual attraction.

I don't mean bare, purely physical, sex-for-pleasure. Sex is a lot bigger than the free sexers ever guess. It's the whole mystery of a man and a woman together. It's the tingling, exciting, can't-sleep-at-night feeling. It's the conversation so exciting you wish you could talk and listen at the same time. It's the drowsy, warm sensation of lying on the grass in the sun just looking at the face of a lover different from anything you dreamed or guessed.

Desire for those feelings will pull you together, again and again. They'll make you want to make love — but if you resist, the energy will go into exploring each other spiritually and mentally. And that will eventually result (if you're really right for each other) in the greatest sex you can imagine.

But what if you do give in? What if you satisfy the drive? Doesn't the sex drive pull you together even more?

In a way, yes. But it won't pull you toward the other person. It'll pull you toward sex. There won't be any deep impulse to bond yourselves to each other for a lifetime — because, as they say, you've gone "all the way." There is (you think and feel) nowhere further to go.

That's why nobody really gets personally involved with a prostitute. Sure, sex drives people back to prostitutes again and again — but for sex, not for prostitutes. Why? Because they go to the end without going through the beginning. The energy of sex is never transferred to the energy of talking, of exploring, of meeting totally as people. A few minutes and it's all over. ALL OVER!

This is especially true for guys. A girl may feel drawn closer by sex. She may say, "I couldn't understand how he acted. It was as though I meant nothing to him once we'd made love." One study showed that for college couples living together with no strings attached, the girls nearly always were hurt much more by breaking up than the guys. It isn't that the guy is cold, necessarily: it's just that he reacts differently.

Really great sex takes time and frustration — more time and frustration than a typical guy (and maybe a typical girl), left to his own instincts, will give it! Quick sex never deals with problems creatively. When something comes between you, you split. Or you use the powerful emotions of more sex to "overcome" the problem. But the problem keeps coming back, and sex becomes a bore. You still aren't really together. Sex doesn't solve problems: it can only express love that has worked to find a solution. And so, without creative problem-solving, love ends up frustrated.

Great sex is the opposite. It endures. It works. It waits for the proper time. And it results in deep freedom for a couple.

Okay, I hear you. You're saying, "But what about marriage? There you get immediate satisfaction for your sex drives. Are you saying that when you have sex with someone it gets boring? If so, why would anyone marry?"

But it's not the same. For one thing,

you don't marry without first taking the time and frustration of getting to know your lover well. Maybe more important is what happens as a marriage grows. In any sexual relationship, the intense sexual excitement eventually lessens. That's true in married sex or free sex. In free sex, it usually leads to a splitting up and a search for renewed thrills elsewhere. The process can become habitual: an endless search for wilder kicks.

A marriage, on the other hand, because of the security and the time it offers, can lead to a deeper lifetime of personal love. Marriage is for two *persons*, not just two people romping in bed. Maybe that doesn't sound so exciting. But find a really happily married couple and ask them if they'd trade it for thrills. No way. Nobody would choose person-less sex over sex with the most fascinating person he has ever known.

Ink and Paper Vows

Another thing is that piece of paper. (Ah, we're finally getting to that piece of paper.) Sure, I know you don't like that. Love should be . . . *love,* for crying out loud! Not ink and paper. True. But ink and paper sometimes help hold the love together.

Take a look at yourself, especially your emotions. You know they change from day to day. Some days the world looks great — others it looks rotten.

That continues even when you're with the dream girl/guy of your life. Some days, married or not, you're going to look at that thing lying beside you in bed, snoring away, and it's not going to look all that attractive. It'll be one of those days when life bores you and you feel stale. And then something is going to whisper in your ear, "Why him?" Or, "Why her? Why this life?" And you'll want like anything to get out of there.

I don't care how stable you are or how wonderful your mate. That day will come. Being bored is part of the human condition. Having sex doesn't cure it: in fact it can intensify it, because it undoes one of the last mysteries in life.

If that boredom comes and there is no

Avow you make to yourself is a lot less likely to have an effect than one you tell everyone about

permanent commitment, you'll probably split. Maybe not that day. That first moment you'll say, "I could never hurt my lover like that."

But there is always the next day. That thought generally takes root in your mind unless you kick it out. It can come back stronger and stronger.

But on that first day, a piece of paper can do you a lot of good. It might shame you enough to kick that thought out of your mind.

Now when I say "piece of paper" I really mean more than that. I mean a wedding. I mean a great celebration you designed yourself and to which all your friends are invited to see this tremendous person you're marrying. I mean a public

solemn promise to God and your friends that nothing is going to get in the way of the two of you, no matter what. And I mean months of planning and thinking about each other and the vows you're going to make.

Aesthetically, I'd say the uniting of two people in love demands a celebration with their friends. It's simply the best way to start life together.

And it has a practical effect. You know yourself that a vow you make to yourself is a lot less likely to have an effect than one you tell everyone about. The first one is simple to change your mind about. The second one is difficult and embarrassing to change your mind about.

And that's good.

It had never occurred to me that my own parents ever had any troubles adjusting. But they did. They told me so.

My mom said an interesting thing: she said even at the worst she never seriously considered packing up and leaving, because she knew that if she went home, her mother would put her on the next train back to my dad. She wouldn't even get a sympathetic ear.

And all her friends would be against her, too. There would be a very simple rule: if she left, no matter who started the fight, it was her fault. If he left, it would be his fault.

So she quickly kicked any thoughts of leaving out of her mind. She's very happy she did, because she'd be in bad shape without my father. And so would he be without her. And I'd be in the worst shape of all!

Changes

So when somebody says that slip of paper means nothing, don't believe it. Maybe a piece of paper you get waiting in line at the marriage bureau means nothing, but the kind you get from a big party with all your friends and family there, followed by a wild honeymoon — that kind means a lot. It can take you over some low spots that the free-sexers never make it past: those times when sex has become ho-hum and you've seen your mate's every fault.

Love that Lasts

I was talking to a kid. He said, "Okay, I agree with you that the very best sex is for marriage. But what's the harm of doing it in the meantime? I know these relationships don't mean that much to me, if I'm honest with myself. I say they'll last forever, but I know they won't.

"But I figure when the right time comes, I'll know it. And then I'll act differently."

Oh, no you won't.

FACT #4: *Habits build up.*

Habits are powerful, and sex habits are the most powerful of all. They don't involve just part of you: they affect your whole way of treating life and people.

Sure, there are cases of persons who straighten up when they meet the right person. They suddenly stop being careless and start really loving someone in the deepest way. They get married and have kids and never mess around again.

But that isn't the norm. Check the statistics on people who don't mind premarital sex and you'll find that, if they ever do get married, they continue to have troubles with sex. Affairs. Divorces. It isn't quite as pretty as it looks in

Wheaton College

There is a kind of love that allows two people to relax and totally be themselves — no threats, no fears, no guilt. It's the kind of love only a "piece of paper" brings.

Playboy. Because habits do build up.

FACT #5: *Real love takes security to grow. Doubt destroys it.*

There is no sex or love so fulfilling as the kind where there is plenty of time, plenty of privacy and no doubt that the person you're with is yours for life. That's not the kind of situation where jealousy and selfishness spring up because of fear. It's the kind of situation where you can relax and be yourself. There's no threat, no fear of guilt, no doubt of the other person's faithfulness, now or 10 years from now. Not even wrinkles and baldness and a lousy figure will hurt your love. It's deeper than that. That's the kind of situation where sex can really go all the way.

FACT #6: *Premarital sex will erode your relationship with God.*

Well, maybe you don't care. If you don't, skip this. But maybe God means a lot to you.

Like a girl who wrote me a letter the other day. She said she and her boyfriend have always had a deep Christian relationship. Maybe they talk about God together. Maybe they pray.

It won't last long. They may still call it a Christian relationship, but it won't be. It will lose the real joys of relating to God. Because you can't listen to what God says and go out and do the opposite too often. Prayer will mean less, and the great Christian sharing times will mean less, and worshipful enthusiasm will mean less. In fact, pretty soon they won't mean anything at all. They'll shrivel up and die a natural death, and you may not even realize they're gone. Except when you wake up in the middle of the night and wonder where God is.

I've seen this happen to some pretty tremendous Christians.

Of course, if you're seeing this happen in yourself, there is a way out. God wants to be your friend. He always will. But sometimes we cut ourselves off from him and make it difficult for him to talk.

And then it's up to us to start communicating again.

All you have to do is say you're sorry. And ask him to help you start acting the way he says.

Don't get me wrong. God doesn't automatically send to hell everyone who slips up with sex. Sex sin isn't too different from lying or jealousy, or a lot of other things. Nor does premarital sex necessarily make you unfit to find the extraordinary love, the great sex-and-love that all of us want. It doesn't. There are always exceptions.

But the odds are stacked against you. Why chance it?

Why settle for the ordinary kind of sex, the kind everyone in this neurotic, spinning world goes for? Why not go for the extraordinary sex-and-love that will last a lifetime?

But don't think you can get it without making a few sacrifices along the way. The runner trains to win a prize. The doctor studies when he's tired enough to drop, in order to save lives. Lovers who want to be the very best have to pay a price, too.

They have to wait. ∎

Ninety per cent of all Americans get married — a lot of them right out of high school. The pressure to get married is so strong you can feel it. But what if you're not yet ready to join that majority? You might want to know . . .

What If I Never Get Married?

Kurt Reichenbach

by Alice Fryling

■Many students cringe at the thought that the "Wedding March" might not follow the "Pomp and Circumstance" of graduation. And through books, TV and advertising, our society constantly tries to convince us that single living is second-rate living. What unclaimed student hasn't asked, "So what's wrong with *me?*"

Much to my delight, the year after graduation proved that these things were not true. That year was one of the biggest surprises of my life — it was fun! And for the following four-and-a-half years, I learned that single living can be absolutely first-rate. It can be a short time or a lifetime of learning, discovering, growing and giving.

I spent that time discovering myself. For instance, I never knew how much I'd enjoy entertaining. I found that I could cook. I could buy my own tires for my car. And I could fill out my own income tax form. That may not sound like much, but these things added up. I could do more than just face life; I could create it.

What a privilege it was to be single and able to dig into activities and friendships that some of my married friends had to miss. I worked on the college Inter-Varsity staff — one of the greatest experi-

Staying Single?

Here are some practical suggestions for living alone and liking it.

1. Get involved in interesting, giving activities. If you have an office job, be sure to spend at least some time each week in "people-oriented" activities where you are meeting someone else's needs.

2. Create a home. Don't wait until you are married to enjoy rugs on the floor, flowers in the window and dinner by candlelight. Your home can become a refuge for others whether you are single or married.

3. Seek to fulfill your role as a woman (or man) even while you are single. Man (or woman) does not reflect the full image of God. (Genesis 1:27) The men you know need your womanly attributes even in the most businesslike relationships; the same is true for women. Seek out relationships where you can offer much as a woman or a man.

ences of my life. I could travel, go on vacations with friends, follow an impulse to pick up and leave town for a weekend, have friends in or stay home alone with a book. Learning to enjoy being alone, as well as being with people, was a great thing.

I must admit that it wasn't all bliss. There were times when the ''What's-wrong-with-me?'' type questions really got me down. I used to tell God, ''If only you'd let me know, I wouldn't mind waiting.'' The uncertainty was hard to take. But it was that uncertainty, that wondering whether or not God wanted me to be permanently single, which led me into the scriptural teaching on the single life. I was surprised at how much the Bible had to say.

Gift of Singleness

Paul is specific in 1 Corinthians 7:7 when he comments that he wished everyone were single as he was, but that ''each has his own special gift from God,'' clearly implying that to be able to stay single is a gift. Paul's comments here cause many people to feel that he is against marriage. But remember that the same man who wrote 1 Corinthians 7 also wrote Ephesians 5 — one of the most exalted views of marriage in all of literature. This is no low view of marriage, only a high view of being single.

In the last half of 1 Corinthians 7, Paul states several principles for single living. He says in verses 17-24 that a man should stay in the state in which he was called by God. I take this to mean, at least in part,

that a single person should not be earnestly seeking marriage. God wants us in the circumstances where he has placed us right now. To plan my life around where and when I can meet the perfect man or woman is to miss the joy of asking God where he wants me and assuming that he will then bring that person to me in his time.

The next principle, in verses 25-35, involves time and priorities. From a very practical standpoint, Paul says that the single person has more time and less anxieties than the married person. There's no getting around it. The beauty of this passage is his positive emphasis. Notice verse 35. Here is the key of the

A single person should not be earnestly seeking marriage. God wants us in the circumstances where he has placed us right now.

single life: not restraint, rejection or second-best, as our society says, but freedom, service and devotion to the Lord. By putting this in the context of a gift from God, Paul implies that these benefits of the single life exist because God chooses to give them to us. And will he not, therefore, also supply all we need for problems that arise because we are single? Any other gift that God gives comes complete with the equipment to use it. Certainly the gift of the single life will be complete too.

What About Me?

As I studied these passages I asked, what is God saying to me? I concluded that I would not get married unless my life plus my husband's life would mean more to the kingdom of God, either in service or in changes of character, than our two lives separately would mean. This was not a lightly-made decision. I wrote it down and shared it with a friend.

This did not mean that I was no longer interested in a husband, nor did it mean that I no longer wanted to get married. But I was submitting these desires to God, trusting that if he gave me the gift of the single life, he would also fulfill my needs.

I believe God did give me the gift of the single life. In my case it was temporary. I am certain he gave me the gift because during my single years I was fulfilled, happy and independent. But when it was time for me to be married, I began to see needs in my life that could only be filled by the man I loved. I didn't leave the single life with a sense of leaving either first-rate or second-rate living. God had called me to one life-style, and now he was leading me into another. How I thank him for them both! ∎

4. Consider your single life an investment. If you are able to be married eventually, it will be an investment into your marriage. If not, it can be an investment into the lives of others who don't have the time to do all that you can do. The time you spend now, learning to sew, cook, paint, play the piano, sing solos or just relate to people, may have multiple benefits in future years. (I am continually thankful for the things I learned while I was single. My single life gave me much more to give my husband.)

5. Remember that we are fighting a battle. Our society is saying one thing: God's Word says another. The ultimate question is, am I going to give in to the strong influence of my society, which says that marriage is the key to happiness, or am I going to trust God who says, "No good thing will I withhold from you"?

It is a war, but I pledge my allegiance to God. He satisfies the desire of every living thing. All the paths of the Lord are steadfast love and faithfulness. He has never failed to keep his word.

One girl had a bad bout with the "Wedding Bell Blues."
Like a lot of people, she wondered . . .

———Can I Be Happy Alone?———

■ As I turned on the light and walked in wearily from the wedding of two friends, the cockroaches scrambled frantically over the sink and counter space to find the dark. The quiet darkness shouted that the newlyweds were on their honeymoon and no longer alone. But I was alone and God had forgotten me. I lay down on my bed and cried tears of self-pity and anger. When the feelings subsided, I found myself challenging God to show me whether a person could be single and fulfilled. That night was the beginning of an adventure.

For as long as I can remember I had assumed that I would someday marry. After all, don't women exist for marriage and for children? Isn't it their destiny under God? It really never entered my mind that I would do anything else. As a teenager I had watched young brides walk the aisles. I saw them as Cinderellas, and wondered when the experience would be mine. It was all so "beautiful," so "white," so "right," so "happily ever after."

This sense that marriage was my destiny was further reinforced as friends of my parents would ask me who I was dating and make inferences about "when you get married" and "when you have

children of your own." Only seldom did the scary thoughts and feelings surface. Then I would ask myself, "What if I'm not one of the lucky ones?" But I would quickly relax, because I didn't really know any unmarried women. If all the people I had met could get married, so could I.

I felt constant pressure during high school to always enjoy a date. Sometimes I wished I had the guts to say, "No, I don't want to go with you, I just want to stay home and read," but I quickly squelched those thoughts. Of *course* I wanted to go to a basketball game, not because basketball was interesting but because life was really only meaningful when you were with a man. It made no difference whether I enjoyed the companionship of the guy. What mattered was that he was a guy and he wanted to be with me. Often I felt uncomfortable as I tried to be whatever I thought a guy wanted me to be. The relationship felt shallow and insincere. *Is this what it will always feel like?*, I pondered.

After becoming a Christian, the religious culture reinforced these feelings. Why not ask God for my future husband? After all, wasn't marriage the reward God sent if you were "a good little Christian

by Heidi Frost

Richard T. Nowitz

girl"? The few unmarried women I met were not excited about their lives. I saw only lonely babysitters, little old ladies with blue hair and tennis shoes who moped around, and parents and neighbors who wrung their hands over their unmarried daughters.

It culminated in that tearful night in my bedroom. From that point, God set me on a new adventure: to find out if I could be single *and* fulfilled. Things began to change once I felt free to share my feelings with God. I told him bluntly about my anger and hostility. It cleared the air between us. I had not really believed God wanted to hear my feelings. How amazing! We are related to a God who cares about what we feel and asks us to share our feelings with him so that we can move into the adventure he has for us. I also discovered God didn't strike me dead or blind when I expressed anger or hurt feelings.

Slowly I began to see the gifts that exist in the single life. Was it possible that being married or being single is just an environment in which one lives one's life? Was it possible that singleness could be good *or* bad, depending on what you made of it?

I shall never forget going home after a

Changes

conference with Bruce Larson, a former colleague on the Faith at Work staff. His wife Hazel had picked him up at the New York airport, and I had gotten on the bus to take the 45-minute ride into Manhattan. I had done this many times. Each time, self-pity would rise as I thought of Bruce's going home to a warm and welcoming family eager to hear about his recent experiences, eager to bring his slippers and a bowl of ice cream. The contrast to my lonely ride home to the cockroaches and a dark apartment was stark. But on this particular night I was even more tired than usual. I realized that all I wanted was to be alone, take a hot bath and fall into bed. Perhaps Bruce wanted to do the same thing. How, I asked myself, will he percieve the people he loves when he is feeling tired and wishing to be alone? Perhaps as baby vultures wanting a piece of him! For the first time in a long time, I relaxed in my seat on the bumpy bus and thanked God for quiet apartments and the gift of going home alone.

As I began to confront my self-pity over being single, the world around me became alive. Jesus became real to me in his humanity. As I read the gospels and lived into his experiences, I took seriously the fact that he was a single man. If he was tempted as I have been, then he knows the frustrations of eating alone and going to bed alone, of not coming "first" with anyone, and of feeling like a third wheel in a culture which understands people best in pairs.

Jesus, too, struggled to claim his personhood above any role he might be put into. Sincere and well-meaning people must have asked him, "You still aren't married?" "How can an attractive person like you still be single . . . ?"

Jesus, though, did not succumb to the pressures. He was secure in his personhood and his belief that God had called him to be who he was. He believed it was okay to take up space in this world *because of who he was,* not because of the roles he filled. Jesus modeled something for me that was becoming a reality in my

Jesus knows the frustrations of feeling like a third wheel in a culture which understands people best in pairs

life. The more I acted on the fact that God loved me because of who I was and not because of the roles I filled (daughter and career person), the more excited I became about discovering myself and the person God created me to be.

I began to recognize the excitement of special gifts the single life offered. My job, for example, gives me the opportunity to travel. I probably would not be doing that were I married. I saw that my abilities would have less opportunity for expression if I lived in a house with two small children. Don't misunderstand me. Lots of gifts can be used with small children, and I see that as an exciting, fulfilling way to live. But I had seen that as the *only* way to live.

I began to look at marriage in a new way. Before, whenever a woman friend had expressed to me stresses in her marriage relationship and feelings of confinement with small children, I had simply mused in a smug way, "Well, my marriage will never be like that . . . I'll be so grateful to be rescued that I'll be glad to raise his children and take care of his needs." My need for marriage at that point blocked me from being realistic.

I thank God that bit by bit I am learning to accept the fact that in whatever state I am, I am okay.

That does not mean there is no pain for me as a single person. I have good days and bad days. Some days the gifts that are a part of my life are evident to me and I feel rich and fulfilled. Other days the realization that I am not first in anyone's life comes crashing in. I'm learning that as a Christian, I can face these painful areas realistically. Fellow Christians are often able to help me meet some of these needs in creative ways.

It has helped me to look beyond other singles for relationships. Older persons, children and married friends offer diversity to my life, and meet some of my needs. All of us are looking for closeness and intimacy. I need (as do all married people) to know that I am important — that I am taken seriously and am valued by other persons. I need closeness in relationships, including the gift of touch. Again, I am amazed at what Jesus models

for me. He was always touching people, realizing how important it was for persons to know that they were cared for in that way. An arm around my shoulder or a hug can bring affirmation and support in a way that words cannot.

I recall a visit that I had recently with a college friend whom I had not seen for years. On my way home to Columbia, Maryland, I stopped over at her invitation. In the midst of peanut butter, toys, baths, skinned elbows and nightmares we had an opportunity to share some of the agonies and ecstacies of the last few years.

At one point, while her children were playing happily and we had a moment of peace, she laughed and said, "I sometimes wonder if life hasn't played a trick on me. I had felt sorry for you, Heidi, because I was the lucky one who had found a husband and you had not. But as I hear about where you've been and see the excitement bubble forth in you, I wonder who's really the lucky one. I struggle with feeling like I'm nothing but a machine for putting on food and diapers and taking kids out of cars and out of the street."

Flying home, I thought a lot about what my friend had said. It felt good to have someone see me as okay. I thought of the long road to freedom I have been traveling as a single person. I was reminded of Paul's words that whatever state he was in, he felt content (Philippians 4:12). The realization came over me that the gift I have from God is contentment in being single. ∎

After high school, questions about marriage come up with surprising regularity. One by one your friends will find their way to the altar, and the subtle pressure to get married begins. Here are one person's down-to-earth answers to help keep your head out of the clouds when wondering . . .

How Do I Find the Right Person?

■ I expected deep and mysterious discoveries about the foggy world of married life. I had decided to write a book based on interviews with 10 couples, whom I would carefully select for their honesty. I figured if I could get 10 couples to really open up and expose what marriage was all about, it could help a lot of people facing marriage.

And so I talked to the couples, probing with the persistence of an acupuncturer. I found plenty of surprises. For one thing, it seems that Christian marriages are bursting with problems and tensions and misunderstandings, just like other marriages. But the biggest surprise was that practically every couple wanted to talk about what happened *before* they were married. No trends popped up unexpectedly in their marriages; the seeds had all been present way back in high school or college when they had started dating.

When I'd bring up a heavy question about their sex life, instead of telling me about the unusual sex tensions in marriage, they told me about how they'd gotten on the wrong track way back in high school. When I searched for inner secrets they had uncovered about each other after marriage, I learned that the signals had all been there before the ceremony —

by Philip Yancey

they had just been too "in love" to heed them.

After listening to all these couples' tales of love and woe, I began thinking. Maybe what's needed even more than a book on how to survive marriage is a good book on how to know what you're getting into. Here are some of the things I learned from my interviews. They're not out of sociology books or religious books on marriage. They're straight out of peoples' lives — my friends who were honest enough to share themselves.

Do You Really Know Each Other?

It seems like a strange question for our day. After all, starting back in junior high, couples pair off and spend every possible second with each other. They dash between classes for a three-minute walk together through the halls. They squeeze every second out of a curfew date. Yet, as one couple told me, "I think we spent more time picking out our wedding bands than thinking about our compatibility."

Love does a strange thing. It makes us feel so good, because we're finally wanted and accepted, that it can blind us to the person who's doing the wanting and accepting. It's not that hard to work up a mushy feeling about a good-looking girl or guy when all you're doing is going bowling, walking the halls together, watching TV, going out to eat. But what is that person really like? Does he or she have qualities which can last through the tensions of raising a family and buying a home and facing illness? Is this really the kind of person you want to spend your life with?

How do you find out about someone? Chances are you can't trust your own judgment completely. Talk to your friends and ask how they think you fit with your partner. If you can swallow your pride, talk to your parents. They'll likely be rougher on a date than anyone else, because they have more at stake. They want the best for you.

If you're really serious, there are professional ways you can find out about each other. Many school counselors and pastors give personality profile tests, like the California test. The tests are fun to take; they make you think about yourself in ways you probably never have. And they don't come up with a "Get married/Don't get married/Neither of the above" answer. They factually point out similarities and differences between you that you should be sensitive to. They

Changes

don't make the decision for you, they merely help you with it.

Another important clue is to figure out what your tastes are like. Will you get bored with each other after two years? One couple told me, "After two years all the romance had worn off and we realized we were totally bored. I like to listen to music on the stereo to relax while Stephanie insists on watching TV cop shows. I like quiet evenings to unwind from a hard day, just reading or listening to music. She always wants to talk or do something manual. I like a simple life — a couple of huge bean bags for chairs, one set of plastic dishes and glasses. Stephanie insists on china and silver and new clothes and stuff. Neither of us wants to give in. The funny thing is, we knew about our tastes before we were married. We just thought it would be different, that somehow love would cover all those things."

Sometimes love in marriage does change people radically. But it's safe to say that the big differences between you now will carry over into your marriage.

One couple I talked with stood out in contrast from the others because their marriage seemed to work so well. They disagreed and fought, like everyone else, but overall they seemed happier and more in love than any others I talked to. I asked them why and the husband said, "I think it's because we agreed on certain principles about our marriage while we were still engaged. We agreed on how far to go in fights and arguments, and on what threats were off-limits. We agreed

to encourage each other every day. And we found that every agreement we made before we were married was 10 times more important than agreements we made after the wedding. Somehow we respected them more. They were a part of our marriage contract."

Is Your Relationship A Trap?

Love, though beautiful, can be dangerous. It can pull you closer to a person than you've ever been before, but it can also wrap tentacles around you and trap you with that person long after you should have split. You can see it in any high school or college. Look around at the couples who spend the most time together. Some of them are sullen and unhappy all the time. Though they make everyone around them miserable, they hang onto each other like man-eating plants locked in embrace. It could be that they're in a trap they don't know how to jump from.

This is a tricky area to talk about with couples, because people don't like having someone shake his finger and say, "Now listen — are you sure it's not time to break up?" We naturally rebel against that kind of preachy tone. So I won't do any preaching — I'll just tell you about the traps mentioned by the couples I interviewed:

▶*The Sex Trap.* Understandably this trap ranked highest on the list. Almost every couple mentioned it in some form. One was particularly eloquent. "Sex was like glue in our relationship. Every time something would rip and tear between us, we never dealt with the problem. We covered it over with glue. It was sweet and sticky, and felt good at the time, but when we were married we were left with a marriage made up of tears and rips. And suddenly sex didn't seem so special anymore. It lost its healing powers."

The sex trap is easy to spot. Do you turn to sex as a cure-all to patching over hurts and misunderstandings? Do you blame a lot of frustrations and tensions on your lack of sexual freedom? Do you allow sex to keep you from other people and other situations which might teach you more about each other?

Does one of you use sex as a weapon to

Look around at the couples who spend the most time together. Some of them are sullen and unhappy all the time — they hang onto each other like man-eating plants locked in embrace.

get his way? Does your partner pressure you with the line that sex is a proof of your love?

You can read preachy advice about sex anywhere, and when you're caught up in the sex trap, it's the most unwelcome advice you'll want to hear. I'll simply say

that these couples told me sex was the biggest liar of all the traps. Sex shouted at them, "See, we are in love. Our affection proves it," all the while keeping them from the honest and hard questions they should have been asking.

One girl's story was tragic. She said, "We had two-and-a-half years of crummy sex. I was always listening for Grandmother's footsteps in the hallway, or peering around a tree to see if anyone was coming, or tensing up when headlights shone on our car. And after three years of marriage, I've lost all sexual desire. I haven't had an orgasm since I've been married."

It doesn't always happen that way, but the sex trap can be deadly.

▶ *The Lemon-squeezer Trap.* Second on these couples' list was the trap that occurs when one partner decides his mission in life is to change the other partner and squeeze out all the bitter, undesirable qualities. Sometimes it's done with the best of Christian intentions.

One guy made it a personal campaign to rebuke his lover every time she was in a bad mood or got angry or criticized someone. He thought he was doing God a favor by improving this girl. Actually he was squeezing her until she broke, and she still hasn't recovered from self-hatred and a horrid self-image. She has a hard time believing anything worthwhile about herself. Before marriage, she took his rebukes more readily, because she wanted him so badly. After marriage, she had no escape.

Another girl nagged at her boyfriend

Rohn Engh

about every picky detail: the muddy shoes he wore, the way he drove the car, his lazy friends, the country church he went to. Now married, he still hasn't flushed out all the built-up resentments against her. He sees her as a nagging burden who takes all the fun out of his life. He looks forward to business trips when he can be away from her.

Each partner has to make certain changes. But if you can't approach those changes in a spirit of love and cooperation, you should break up. One man said he had a miserable marriage for 13 years. Then one day he learned to stop saying, "If you love me you will . . ." and said "Because I love you I will . . ."

A human being you take on to love is a fragile, delicate thing.

Everyone needs support and affirmation. Marriage can be the best environment of support or the worst, depending on how you approach it.

▶*The Pity Trap.* Watch this one closely, because love and pity can be easily confused. One guy I interviewed grew up in a sad home where his mother would shout and abuse him. His girl friend sprang to the rescue, and would lovingly soothe him and build him up. That was great. But the whole relationship became based on his girl friend's concern for him. He enjoyed her attention and affection

Marriage is full of shocks and surprises you'll never be completely ready for. But find out all you can about each other; that'll prepare you better than anything.

and never saw his own responsibility to try to meet *her* needs. It was a one-sided romance, and the problem still recurs in their marriage.

God can use love to heal broken families. But marriage is give-and-take, and both people must contribute or it will die. If your romance is based on pity, you're walking on thin ice.

The April '75 issue of *Seventeen* contained an article by a psychologist who listed all the types of guys that are poor risks for a girl to marry. His list included the mama's boy, the guy who has bruising battles with his family, the guy who uses romance as an escape from his problems and the guy who is always rebelling against something, thinking he has been wronged. Each one of those situations can develop into the pity trap.

Marriage is tough, hard and adult. Pity is not a strong enough emotion to withstand it.

How Do You Face Crises?

This is a hard question to answer for many unmarried couples. Your life can be fairly sheltered. If you live at home, you probably haven't run into tough financial decisions. Unless there's been an accident or illness, it's hard to know how you will face a crisis.

But marriage does involve crises, and it's good to think about how your partner could respond. If one partner is nervous, insecure and panicky under pressure, the other should learn to balance those feelings.

One important question to ask is, *Do we turn to each other under pressure or does pressure split us apart?* (A related and very important question for Christian couples is, *Does pressure turn us toward God, or do we resentfully turn away from Him?*)

One couple faced a damaging blow after two years of blissful marriage. The girl came down with Hodgkin's disease, cancer of the lymph glands. Suddenly a dark cloud covered all their plans. He had to care for her constantly, postpone his college, manage the house, keep money coming in and be strong emotionally. She had to face the 50-50 chance of death. It

You can't clam up in marriage; you've got to stay open and be willing to share, even when it hurts. Those who learned to do that in the dating stage had an advantage when marriage came.

was a heavy experience for a young couple.

The girl was cured after two years of painful treatment, and their marriage survived stronger than ever. Why? "I worked as a chaplain's assistant at a hospital," John said, "and I saw the way couples handle crises. In movies like *Airport*, when it looks as if the plane will crash, couples who have been quarreling for years suddenly hug each other and forgive. Life isn't like that. If you're in the pattern of turning to each other and supporting each other, you'll do the same thing in a crisis. The pressure and heat will weld your love to make it thick and firm. If you're in the pattern of pulling apart and feeling sorry for yourself . . . the crisis can open up permanent wounds."

Crises are a good sieve to screen out mushy, weak love. True love flourishes when one partner is needy.

One other thing — don't underestimate the value of money. Most surveys report that well over half the marriages which break up within two years do so because of money disagreements. Make it a point to find out how your partner feels about money, and decide mutually on what kind of life-style you want to lead.

Do You Have These Qualities?

When I asked these couples what qualities were most important to them in their marriage, there was surprising agreement. Everyone admitted communication was very important. You can't clam up in marriage; you've got to stay open and be willing to share, even when it hurts. Those who learned to do that in the dating stage had an advantage when marriage came.

Honesty was mentioned next. Marriage can be devastating, because it destroys your secrets. When you live with a person so intently, it's hard to hide things. Dishonesty puts a wedge between you.

Words like tolerant and flexible and considerate surfaced often. Those couples who went into marriage with firmly cemented ideas of what it would be like usually were surprised. The coming together of two people forms a living, growing organism of marriage. You both will change, your relationship will change and you need to be prepared to adapt.

Love, of course, was most commonly mentioned. Most couples went to great pains, however, to point out that their idea of love changed immensely after marriage. The concept became much less romantic and more practical. For the best description of the love they mentioned, read 1 Corinthians 13 in the Bible. It's not the kind of love you see in movies and on TV, but it's the kind that can make a marriage.

One encouraging note. After reading about all these problems and disagreements and surprises, your head may be swimming. *I'll never find a relationship that meets all those characteristics,* you may be saying. Cheer up. You'll never be fully prepared for marriage. It's bound to bulge with surprises. The important thing is to know your partner well, and make sure you're in God's will.

Remember, all the couples who shared these problems are still married. Most describe themselves as happily married. They merely shared their problems to help you avoid the same pitfalls. ∎

Jobs

Whether you go on to college or set out to carve your niche in the world, you'll more than likely be needing a job. It helps support that costly habit we call life.

The following articles deal with various aspects of finding, getting and keeping jobs — from part-time jobs to help out with pocket money and college expenses, and beyond, to choosing your future career.

David S. Strickler

Maybe you're ready to hold down the first regular job you've ever had. Most people after high school find that some kind of job is a necessity. But if you're new to the game you need to know . . .

How Can I Find a Job?

by Steve Lawhead

■ You know something's up when your mother starts billing you for meals and laundry, your father always seems to be humming "Nothin' But a Bum" whenever you're around, and lately your grandmother shows an uncommon familiarity with the word "lazy." Gradually the dawn breaks — it's time to get a job!

Now the work begins. It's not a matter of walking into a place of business and saying, "Here I am, what do I do?" Those days — if there ever were days like those — are gone. In fact, finding a job today may be the hardest work you'll have to do. And you may as well know it, a high-schooler stands at the tail end of the unemployment line, with college-agers just ahead. The job market is tighter than clenched teeth. You'll more than likely find yourself shoulder-to-shoulder with an army of applicants in active competition for any job you seek.

That's the bad news. Now the good news — there *are* jobs available for people who will work to get the job they want and work to keep it. John Adams, director of career services at Grinnell College in Iowa, says that a person's employability "depends much more on *how* a person looks for a job than it does on the economy or your particular background."

Looking Before Leaping

First and foremost on every job-hunter's mind should be what kind of job he is seeking. Many factors come into consideration here, and you may have to do some juggling before you arrive at your final job definition. Consider prior work experience, any job-related skills you may have — such as typing or bicycle repair — how much money you need, the time you can give a job, personal interests you wish to pursue. After all these things are weighed and balanced, you should have a rough idea of the kind of job you want. And don't assume that because you're easy to get along with, a job doing "anything" will work. While it may suit you, it won't suit your boss — people are seldom hired to do just *anything*.

Look at it from a boss's point of view: all the jobs he or she has to offer are important. They all have specific, necessary responsibilities. Usually, a person who'll do anything is not discriminating enough for him — not when competition among job hunters allows him to be choosy. Therefore, learn all you can about the job (or the kind of job) you're seeking. That helps in two ways: it lets the people you will be dealing with know that you are serious, and it narrows down your objective (getting a job, for example) to a more manageable size (like working in a retail store).

Once you've set your sights, make sure they aren't too low. Even in a part-time job, why get locked into a dead-end grind and waste a whole summer in tedious boredom? Select a job that will give you a challenge and keep you on your toes, something you're not already over-qualified for, something where you can learn while you earn. That means you have to be willing to skip over a few offers if they're not anything near what you want. Just because you can do a job doesn't mean you should take it. To accept a job solely for money — even for a summer or part-time job — is foolish.

Pavement Pounding

Armed with a job objective, and with expectations reasonably set, you're ready to hit the streets. This is the most frustrating and depressing part of job hunting — just finding an opening.

First things first. You can always start right where you are, at home, among your family and friends. Anyone you know is fair game. Tell them you're hunting for a job and ask them to let you know if they hear of anything. Don't be afraid to ask anyone. Job hunting is a game of coincidence, and the more "feelers" you have out, the better.

Help-wanted ads in the newspaper are another good starting source. From a purely informational stand-point, they indicate what the general job market is in your locale. As far as specific jobs are concerned, a want ad can show you what the

"going rate" in the salary department is likely to be, what experience you'll need and what benefits you can expect. Bear in mind, however, that *everyone* reads the classified ads. Your most intense competition will come for jobs that have been listed in the newspaper.

Your first venture outside home should be to the state employment agency. These agencies exist to help you; they have the information and trained counselors to answer any questions you might have. A state agency's services are free. Take advantage of them and let them work for you. You will need a Social-Security number just to get beyond the formalities. (You need one if you're planning on working anyway.) If you do not have one, get yourself over to the nearest post office and fill out the necessary forms.

State employment agencies, you'll find, have one big advantage over news-

Job hunting is a game of coincidence, and the more "feelers" you have out the better

paper want ads. Many employers, allowing the state agency to do their preliminary interviewing for them, do not list their openings in the paper. Therefore, the state agency will have knowledge of openings you wouldn't find any other way. They can also help you put together the information you will need for an interview. They will send only one applicant at a time to any given opening, so you needn't worry about someone else beating you to the employer's doorstep. In short, the state agency is a very impartial, helpful source that probably knows as much about the job market in your location as any single entity.

Along with state agencies, there are private employment agencies. They work for a fee, paid by you or the employer. The fee is usually based on any earning you make in the job you take. Most of these agencies are on the up and up, but many are questionable and you could get "burned" very easily. Although private agencies tend to offer the better-paying, hard-to-find or "glamour jobs," they should be considered as a last resort to be used when you have exhausted all other sources on your own. They seldom list part-time jobs or consider high-school students for full-time employment.

Another tool to find openings is personal canvassing — pounding the pavement. This is where you find a place where you'd like to work and go in "cold turkey" to ask for a job. It might surprise you to learn that many department stores, clothing stores and others never advertise an opening, but depend upon this type of approach to fill their vacancies.

While personal canvassing can be nerve-wracking and uncomfortable for some, it has certain advantages. You stumble across some very fortunate circumstances: the firm may have had a position just open up and not yet listed it with anyone. They may be temporarily short-handed and ask you to help out (temporary jobs have a way of extending themselves indefinitely — especially for willing workers). They may be considering a replacement and think you look too good to lose. They may not even know they need someone until you suggest it. (Believe it or not, I once got one of my best jobs this way. The boss wasn't even considering hiring anyone until I brought up the subject. As he thought about it, it occurred to him that yes, he did need someone and I promptly went to work.) Some firms are always on the lookout for energetic people and will hire when they see someone they like. Give it a try. Get out and talk to the people who know about the job you're after. Even if they don't hire you, they can give you invaluable information which can eventually lead to your employment.

If you're long on time and short on transportation, a good way to cover ground fast is with the telephone. Suppose you've decided you want to work in a greenhouse; simply sit down with the yellow pages and go through all the listings under florists. After you've asked to speak to the manager, give him or her your pitch (pre-planned, of course). If the manager's interested, he or she will still want to meet you in person, but it's still saving you a lot of time — not to mention gasoline expenses.

Goose Chasing

Unless you are an exceptionally lucky

person, you probably won't get the first job you apply for — nor the second or third. Weeks will go by without so much as a nibble on your line. You may be rejected so many times you'll feel like joining the foreign legion to forget. There will be hundreds of phone calls made and miles walked just tracking down possibilities, and the natural tendency is to become disheartened, depressed and disgusted. That's okay; you can feel those things, but don't give up. Remember — job hunting is a full-time occupation. To get a good job you have to work very hard, and keep working. And don't panic — that's the second worst thing you can do. Fear of not finding a job can make you take a job you really don't want, or ruin your confidence in an important interview.

Speaking of interviews, everything you have done up to now leads to an interview. An interview is a conversation between you and your prospective employer about you, your experience, your goals and, of course, the job. As a preliminary to the interview, there will be forms to fill out — be sure to bring a pen and all the other materials you will need to fill out an application. Prepare a list of names, addresses and phone numbers of all past employers and at least two other references, the dates you worked, why you quit — everything. Be prepared to answer any questions about your past employment and why you want this job.

Everything you do in the interview should present yourself in the most favorable light. You will be nervous; that's natural. Try to appear poised, self-confident, polite and straight. Arrive at the interview on time (early doesn't hurt), neat, clean and looking like you conform — don't wear any way-out clothing or hair styles. Plat-form wedgies and rhinestone-studded jeans with 26-inch bells and a see-through shirt, pukka shells and a blond-streaked Afro wig are not proper attire for an interview with anybody (except, perhaps, a circus ringmaster). You must convince the interviewer that you are skilled and knowledgeable, reliable, responsible, cooperative and that you are worth the money the job pays. That's hard to do if he is rolling on the floor in uncontrollable, hysterical laughter. Just be yourself as much as possible and if you have any doubts about what to wear — or whether that shirt or dress is clean enough to wear one more time — wear something else. It's nearly impossible to overdress. Don't wonder whether a tie or dress is necessary — wear it.

The specific job you are applying for is bound to come up in the interview. You must have at least a little knowledge of that position, even if you've never held it before. That's where your homework comes in. Don't try to bluff your way into a job, or fake experience you haven't had. That's dishonest and embarrassing, to say the least, and the boss always finds out sooner or later.

A discussion of salary is sure to enter into any serious interview. In fact, you know you've got a good chance at the job when the question of salary comes up. A firm usually will not discuss pay with anyone they are not seriously considering hiring. Whatever you do, don't bring it up yourself. Let the interviewer begin the discussion. If you are in a bargaining position, let him make the first offer. If you don't qualify for the job, obviously salary won't even be discussed. (However, if you *do* get the job and the interview comes to a close and no one has mentioned anything about wages — by all means bring it up. Don't leave the interview without knowing.)

After you've gone through everything, and still don't get the job, keep trying. The next interview and the next will go easier. In fact, if you have a particular firm you want to interview with, it isn't a bad idea to "practice" interviews with several other employers before you go into the one you really care about. That gives you a little experience and you get the questions and answers all worked out. Be patient — interviewing is a time-consuming process — some interviews can eat up half a day. Be prepared for that whenever you accept an interview.

Finding an opening and getting through an interview always involve a lot of wild goose chasing, pavement pounding and sheer determination. This article has hit on only a few of the highlights. Whole books have been written on the subject — most of them are extremely helpful and all of them are far more detailed than this brief article. You can find them in any library or bookstore. The more you know about looking for a job, the better your chances of landing the job you want. Even if it's only a summer job, the experience you get will be worth it. Happy hunting. ∎

David S. Strickler

Learn all you can about the job you are seeking. Don't try to fake experience you haven't had – the boss always finds out.

Just finding a job isn't enough — once you're hired you have to work at keeping it. Unfortunately, every job can't be a dream job. You may have to put up with your share of crummy jobs before you land "The Job." In the meantime . . .

How Do I Handle a Rotten, Lousy

■ I've had a lot of jobs. Most of them you wouldn't consider "glamour" jobs by any stretch of the imagination. At various times I've fixed bikes in a repair shop, delivered pizzas, sodded lawns and planted underground sprinkler systems, changed the movie marquee at a theater, sold shirts in a men's clothing store and detassled corn. None of these jobs were my first choice — if I'd had a choice I'd have done something else, like being a congressman's aide in Washington or a ski instructor at Aspen. But I needed the money. Funny how you can always use an extra dollar.

Some of those jobs were deathly dull, some were exhausting and some jobs put me into contact with irate customers or belligerent bosses. However, they all had one thing in common — plain hard work. That, along with terrible working conditions, made some pretty lousy jobs.

As a working student you begin to understand how it was that the Indians came up with the idea for the totem pole. Since you're the low man on it, you often feel like you have to hold up more than your share of the weight. Generally speaking, the kinds of jobs available to a student aren't designed to always be fair,

comfortable or convenient. They are designed to get the most work done for as little money as it takes — never mind about the human being doing the job. It's grim, but that's the world of the part-time job.

Recently I interviewed high-school students about their part-time jobs to see how they coped. I found out most people aren't coping very well — when things get tough they quit. That's one way to handle a lousy job, but it's not always the best way, especially when you realize it's becoming crucial nowadays to establish a good work record from the very beginning if you want a good job later on.

The Big Bad Boss

One of the chief villains is the boss who's never understood that slavery went out with the Emancipation Proclamation. These modern-day slave drivers can be a big pain. No matter what you do or how hard you work, there's always something more you could have done. How do you deal with a boss who thinks he owns you, body and soul, just because he pays you $2.05 an hour to wait on tables or pump gas?

Getting along with a boss like that will

Part-time Job?

Inland Steel Company

take some effort on your part. Try to understand him; try to understand the job from his point of view. He may be overworked himself; making others work harder could be the only way out of his predicament that he can see. Or he may be afraid; a lot of bosses are afraid their business will fail. Working harder is how they try to cope with that fear.

Regardless of why he's playing the part of Simon Legree, you can go a long way toward making things easier on yourself by earning his trust. Once a boss knows he can trust you to be on time, do a good job and take some responsibility, he'll usually go easier on you. That might mean extra work for you (volunteering for extra hours, coming in early, double-checking your work, etc.) but in the long run it'll pay off. Don't be afraid to point out to him what you're doing for him (he may not notice otherwise). Even if he doesn't give you a raise, he'll appreciate you more.

Boring, Boring, Very Boring

Many jobs require you to do the same thing over and over again, others merely to "be there" in case something happens. Boredom usually takes over on the job

Jobs

How do you survive in a job environment weighted against kids, with generally lousy conditions? Here are three kids who found some practical answers to the question . . .

How Can I Make My Job Better?

Philip Yancey

Steve Henry, delicatessen counter helper

Sometimes I think employers hire teenagers just so they'll have someone to blame when something goes wrong. We're paid terrible wages, given the dirtiest jobs, then used as a scapegoat for everyone else's mistakes. When a mistake is uncovered, it's always, "Ask the kid if he did it."

I ran smack into this during my second week on the job. I was still in the stage of trying to impress everyone with my eagerness, and as far as I knew, I hadn't made any serious blun-

when you've learned to do what you're supposed to do and there are no more challenges. Without the stimulation of a challenge, or an outside diversion, the brain goes to sleep. The struggle in a dull job is really with yourself — how can you stay awake?

Contrary to what you might think, most bosses know when a job is boring. Few would object if you brought a radio from home to help while away the hours. Sometimes you can even bring homework or read a book while you're on the job. The thing to remember is you should be able to demonstrate your ability to handle the job first, before you ask for any special privileges.

Crummy Conditions

Barney Quandt of St. Charles, Illinois, works part-time in a cement-packaging plant. He stacks 90-pound bags of cement, one on top of another, all day long. The work is tedious and exhausting. It's performed in a dirty warehouse where the dusty, powder-filled air makes breathing next to impossible . . . and, there's no drinking water available. Under those conditions most new guys on the job don't last more than one day. How did Barney manage to make it through the entire summer to continue part-time during the fall?

"I could have quit," says Barney, "but I've always been taught that you don't quit something when the going gets rough." That job has developed a lot of self-respect in him; that's what kept him going back day after day to a job he really didn't like.

In a lot of jobs where conditions aren't the best there's a tendency to rely solely on your weekly paycheck to give you a reason to stay. This "I'm-only-in-it-for-the-money" attitude can be destructive in the long run. First of all, you very easily fall into slipshod working habits,

---

Ten Do's and Don'ts for Making Your Boss Glad He Hired You

- Do your best always, even in the minor details.
- Don't talk about your boss behind his back.
- Do show up ready for work, on time and on the days you agreed to work.
- Don't hang out with friends who drop by while you're working.
- Do ask questions whenever necessary.
- Don't bring your personal problems to work with you.
- Do make an effort to get along with fellow employees.
- Don't lie to your boss or cover up for mistakes.
- Do take responsibility for your work; let your boss know he can trust you.
- Don't take anything for granted or leave anything to chance; when in doubt — double-check.

---

ders. But one day my boss took me aside and told me the owner wanted me fired! He didn't have a reason; he just didn't like me. My boss stuck up for me to the owner, and they decided to give me a chance to prove myself. The pressure from then on was unbelievable.

My first reaction was to quit. How could I come to work every day knowing that the owner was just itching for a chance to fire me? I was angry at the blind injustice. And yet I needed the job. My father was disabled, and my family depended on the money I brought home.

I went home and prayed about the whole situation. God helped me get some fresh insight. I could honestly say that the owner was totally at fault — I had done nothing to deserve his wrath. So why should I act like I had done something wrong by quitting in a huff? Why not try to prove to my employers that I could be a conscientious, hardworking employee they could count on?

By nature, I'm rather shy, and it was difficult to show up at work the next day. So I prayed for strength and tried to act cheerful. Whenever the owner walked past me, I'd smile and speak to him. And I even came in after hours, without pay, to help clean up. Gradually I built a foundation of trust, and the owner accepted me.

I learned a lot from that experience. If I had quit in disgust, even with good reason, I'd be out a job, plus I'd have bitter feelings. God taught me that sometimes the best way to handle a situation where you're wronged is to just swallow hard and take it, asking him for the help you need.

Don't think for a moment that God eliminates all the unpleasantries from a job. One customer threw a package of hot dogs at me because he thought the prices were too high! And slopping a mop across supermarket floors will never be glamorous. But I think a Christian kid does have an advantage at work. After all, he's got Someone to turn to when he needs help. He's not alone.

Philip Yancey

Elesia Jackson, dry-cleaning attendant

When I first started, my job sounded clear and simple. I was to work at the counter in a cleaning store, assembling people's dry-cleaning orders and bringing them to the front when the customer showed up. But even the simplest jobs can turn into nightmares when you're dealing with people.

I still can't believe the number of people who come in without their claim tickets. They act like it's my fault they lost their ticket, and I have to go through every article of clothing on the rack till we come to theirs. One day I went through every bag in the entire store with a grumpy man before he remembered he had left his clothes at a different cleaners!

Another time a lady came in with a zipper she wanted us to repair on a cheap dress. We did our best, but she wasn't satisfied. She blew up and started shouting and fuming right in the middle of the store. I tried to calm her down by being understanding and soothing, and finally she did stop yelling. On the way out, after talking to the manager, she stopped by my counter and you begin thinking less of yourself. Soon a feeling of "they can't pay me enough to do this" takes over.

I fell into that when I worked for a company that put in underground sprinkler systems. We worked all day in the hot sun, down on hands and knees digging little holes in the turf. I quickly got discouraged and lived every day only for my check on Friday. Soon, even that wasn't enough. I'd come home from work every day and pour through the want ads looking for a better job. I never found one, so every morning I'd drag myself back to work, dreading every minute of it.

Even though I needed the money for college, I came very close to quitting several times. One day a new guy showed up at work. He joined our crew and suddenly the work didn't seem so bad anymore. This guy brought a lot of self-respect to his job. It didn't mattter to him that the conditions were rotten, or the work was insanely tedious. He acted as if he were there just to do the best job he could do, no matter what. His attitude soon infected the rest of the crew, and we all began working as though that job were the only thing that mattered. It infected our boss, too. He began handing out compliments and buying cokes for us as though there were no tomorrow. I never thought about quitting again, and what's more, when payday rolled around we all picked up our checks with a feeling of pride — it was money well earned for a job well done.

and apologized. That was kind of a triumph for me.

What do I do to relieve the tedium of my job? Well, fortunately I work with two or three other girls my age. You can make a dull job more enjoyable by working with people. Team work helps. Sometimes at the cleaners we work together on jobs that one person could really handle, just to break the monotony.

Before I got involved with Campus Life I had trouble relating to people, because I was angry and bitter. Now I've seen that kids can love and get along without a lot of gossiping and competition. So, using my Christian friends as a model, I try to let God work through me to make *me* the type of person others enjoy being around.

Working has taught me another thing — to appreciate the people who spend their lives trapped in jobs that are just part-time hassles for most of us kids. I don't think I could stand working at the cleaners one day longer if I knew I might be stuck here the rest of my life. It's only a temporary job to help save for college expenses. But a lot of people, including some of my employers, may have boring jobs like this for years.

Now I think twice before I go into a grocery store and yell at the cashier for being slow, or grumble about high prices to someone who had nothing to do with the price increases. I try to put myself in other people's places. I want to be the one to brighten their day and make it a little more bearable.

Jobs

Philip Yancey

Cathy Rowe, fried-chicken salesgirl

I only work part-time, and I'm still in high school, but I've already gotten an ulcer from my job!

Until you've told the fifteenth person in line that he'll have to wait 20 minutes for his fried chicken and french fries, you have no idea how angry grown adults can get. Some stalk out, mumbling. Some yell at one of us cashiers; others sit right in front of the counter and stare us down. I used to take things like that personally, bacause the customers made me feel it was my fault. They have no idea how difficult it is to plan food when you don't know how many people may show up at a certain time. If we cook too much in advance, it gets wasted, or sits around until it tastes terrible.

After the tension and frustrations got to me and gave me an ulcer, my parents wanted me to quit. But I thought it was

You Can Be Replaced

The world of the part-time job is filled with slave-driving bosses, crazy hours, low pay and crummy conditions. You'll likely encounter a combination of one or more of these no matter where you work — it's a law of nature.

In trying to to put up with all of that it helps if you can get some perspective. One point of perspective was shared with me by a friend of mine. He said, "In a part-time job you are paid for how easy you are to replace, not necessarily for how hard the work is." In other words, waitresses and busboys, who are very easy to replace, make a lot less money than someone who is a library attendant. A busboy certainly works harder but students qualified for library work are few and far between; their boss wants to hang on to them, so they get paid more.

This tricky bit of economics, if you think about it, should help you get rid of any inflated notions about how valuable you are to your employer. A busboy who thinks he's too good to bus tables, or isn't paid enough to do it, is going to have problems. You can't work with an attitude like that. It just eats on you until you quit and find a job somewhere else. The only trouble is that wherever you go the same economic principle is involved. Once you accept your situation you can get along with almost anything.

Another perspective I've found most helpful in all the jobs I've had was the advice, "Don't take it too seriously." Deceptively simple, this advice is worth digging into.

On the surface it helps you deal with the day-to-day nitty-gritty of working. Suppose the boss yells at you for making a mistake on the job. Instead of getting angry or holding your resentment inside, give yourself a break. Mistakes happen; if it was your fault admit it and determine to do better next time.

Learning not to take your job (or yourself) too seriously also puts your attitude toward working in the proper perspective. Students who work often get deeply involved with their jobs. They forget about their larger lives away from the job. They seem to do little more than eat, go to school and work. Live a little. Even if the job is unbearable, remember it's only temporary — you won't be trapped there forever. Keep up on your outside interests in your off hours; that'll make the job easier to take. Also, it doesn't hurt to spend a little money on yourself from what you make on the job. Most people don't have much trouble with this, but some do. Treat yourself to something (even a movie or a banana split will do) when the work week is over; it'll make you feel you've earned something.

Of course, if you've got a job that is pure misery and you're sure there's nothing you can do about it, you should probably quit. That's best for everyone concerned. But most on-the-job hassles can be enormously improved by the right attitude. Think of each job as a chance to learn something about the working world and about yourself. If you do that you'll find you can put up with almost anything. ■

important to learn how to handle tension, so I talked them into letting me stay on. Instead of just reacting emotionally to each crisis, I started thinking of ways to cope. For example, if I saw a busload of people coming to the door, I'd quick ask God to give me an extra spurt of energy to remain cheerful. If people had to wait for their chicken or fries, I'd offer them a free Coke and strike up a conversation with them.

When we're caught up and between customers, I've found time passes much faster if I keep busy. Sometimes I have races with myself, timing how long it takes to sweep part of the floor or scrub a stainless steel machine.

As I gained self-confidence, I really began to enjoy what could have been a dull job. I was promoted to train all new helpers, and have stayed at the same job for two whole years. Gradually I began to realize that I had just been playing roles, the "Have a nice day" cashier role, for instance. I concentrated on meaning it when I talked to customers. They can sense when you're sincere.

Over the months we've developed a regular clientele. One couple used to come in drunk and grouchy every few nights. I made a special point to ask them about their interests and how they were doing. Now they come in with a big smile during slow hours so we can talk over whatever problems they might be having. It probably sounds silly to say you can affect people behind a fried-chicken counter, but it's true. God can use you anywhere. ■

**If things get too bad on the job front
and you long for the day when you can be your own boss and
work your own hours . . . what are you waiting for?**

_____Why Not Mind Your Own

Rick Kotter

Business? by Stephen Erickson

■ Are you tired of reading the want ads and finding the same part-time jobs — like heaving hamburgers in your local fast-food franchise? Or pumping gas every day in all kinds of weather, including -20°? Or developing premature varicose veins as a waitress or clerk? If interesting part-time jobs seem almost extinct, maybe you should mind your own business.

Being in business for yourself means you can do what you want and you're completely on your own. Minding your own business can pay off.

One way to start is to find a "service" which people need. Think of work you can do for someone — like mowing the lawn or teaching music — and you're in business!

If you like the outdoors, try yard work. Younger kids used to have a monopoly on the mowers, but in recent years the yard has become unclaimed territory. With a minimum of equipment you should be able to drum up a profitable landscaping or weed-removal business.

Let your imagination run wild over services you could possibly render. "Sitting" services may sound corny, but one college guy organized his sitters so well he made $8,000 in one year. People are always looking for reliable persons to watch their kids. And other things need watching as well.

Some people treat their pets like children. They are very protective about their animals and would rather leave them in the care of a dependable human than in the dark, damp recesses of the town's kennel (which charges up to $5.00 a day). In some towns which have no place to board animals, a pet-sitting service would be in great demand.

Many people regard their plants as part of their family and hate leaving them behind when they go on long trips. If you're up on the care and feeding of plants, plant-sitting might prove profitable also.

House sitting is another possibility, especially during the summer months when people take off on long vacations. Offer to watch a family's house while they're gone, making it look as though they were still on the premises. For instance, pick up their newspapers, keep their mail in a safe place, cut their grass, feed their goldfish, water their plants, etc.

A special talent or skill can prove profitable. Do you play a musical instrument? Private music instruction is a good job, especially if you can teach piano or

Jobs

guitar. If you're a typist, there's always work to be found. Maybe you have a special knack for cutting hair.

Clowns, Cars and Cakes

By reading a few books on magic and joining a magic club, you can make yourself available for entertainment at children's parties. Or if you're a person who likes to clown around, why not make a profit with your antics? A funny clown is a great asset to kids' birthday parties. Get paid for having fun.

Maybe cars are your thing and you possess surgical skill with a lug wrench. People are always on the look-out for dependable car service. You could set up a business changing oil and filters in cars, plus giving a lube job. And how many people who like their cars shiny like to put time and muscle into wax jobs?

If these businesses are too mundane for you, try a more unusual way to make a buck.

Students in the Midwest ran a "pall bearing" company. When funeral homes needed a little help, they called the guys to carry coffins in turn for a good wage.

A couple of students in a rural area made a small fortune customizing mailboxes. For a base price they'd stencil in the owner's name. Any painted decorations were extra. Your paintbrush doesn't have to stop at the mailbox. People's property often needs a coat of paint. There are always porch pillars or trim around the house, wrought-iron touchup, garage doors or even a whole house.

A college group found out the birth-

Being your own boss doesn't mean having all the free time you want – just the opposite. You'll probably work harder than you ever dreamed to make your business a success.

days of every student on campus. They sent letters home to the parents, saying that for five bucks they'd make sure their son or daughter got a cake on his or her birthday. What parent wouldn't give his homesick kid a cake on his birthday?

One guy discovered there's one thing weekend sailors don't like about their cabin cruisers — upkeep. Wooden hulls have to be sanded and refinished regularly. Even the fiberglass ones need a good scrubbing now and then. So the guy visited a few marinas and started a boat-washing company. Not only did he make enough money for himself, he made enough to pay a three-man crew. Eventually boats led to other things. His "company" took a step up and hit the local airport. The crew contracted to wash a passenger plane in turn for a sizable sum.

T-Shirts and Elves

The second route you can take in starting your own business is "product." It's a bit more risky than the service business but can pay off. Can you make a tangible object and sell it? Something like a lint roller? Maybe a fishing lure? How about picnic tables?

One guy noticed the first tides of a craze. Students were just starting to wear imprinted T-shirts. Because it was a craze, he had to work fast — but he didn't cut any corners.

First, he checked to see if he could produce imprinted shirts cheaply and in quantity. By renting a factory owner's machine at night when it wasn't in use, and buying a bulk of cheap, white T-shirts, he found he could undercut anyone else in the area producing similar shirts.

Then he bargained with local sports stores, novelty shops and any other possible outlets for his product. Eventually he advertised in the papers. When things got rolling, his shirts were selling like crazy in stores, and quantity orders were coming directly to him from clubs, bowling teams and other groups. He managed to keep up on his orders, and by the end of the summer had enough money to pay for a year's schooling.

Other youthful entrepreneurs who went the product route came up with some interesting ideas. One guy could handle a jigsaw and paintbrush pretty well. He made two-dimensional lawn figures of elves, dwarves, animals and anything else under the sun. Another guy sold nature photographs that he took and printed himself. His sister made leather book covers and belts.

Another guy was a good artist with a touch of wit. He made and sold caricatures at shopping centers. A high-school girl made needlepoint pillows.

By now you've probably thought of other ideas for your own business. Just remember a few words of parting advice. There's no guarantee that you'll make it. Your own business doesn't necessarily mean job security. Also, ask your parents or school counselor about income tax and small business laws. And be prepared to work a little. Your own business is only as successful as you make it. ∎

As you think about your future and how you'll spend it, there may be an answer you've overlooked . . .

Why Not Work Overseas?

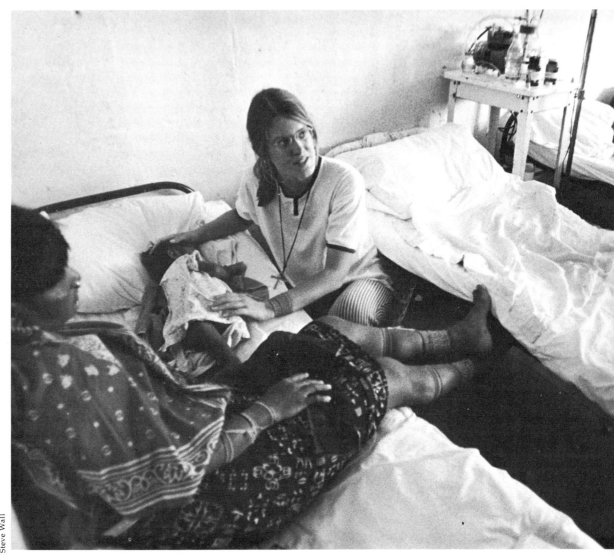

by Tim Stafford

■ I remember the days when life was simple and all we worried about was a nuclear holocaust. In Lyndhurst, New Jersey, they used to turn on the air-raid sirens every other Saturday afternoon at 2:00, just testing. You could go see displays of the latest portable bomb shelters at shopping centers. I was pretty young then, but my impression is that people were genuinely scared. When those sirens went off on Saturday we would look at the clear blue sky and wonder what might come out of it next. There was more to the Fifties than saddle shoes.

The Sixties had their own fears: you could get sent to Vietnam if you were a certain age. Or the cities might go up in smoke. Or the nation might disintegrate in a leftist youth rebellion.

The great fear choking the Seventies seems to be *will I get a job?* It's strangling colleges with eager-beaver students studying twice as hard as they used to. Their study habits don't seem motivated by a desire to learn more, or a love of the material. The motive seems to be raw fear — fear that *if I don't work hard enough, I might not get a job*. I talk to kids who have everything going for them yet seem miserable because they don't yet know what they are going to do with their lives.

Those fears seem silly to me, at least in comparison to a nuclear holocaust. Most Americans do end up in work that is at least tolerable. And your chances of getting a good job have more to do with becoming an intelligent, balanced, enjoyable person than they do with raising your grade-point average a couple of points.

But beyond that, those fears strike me as being anti-Christian. The first reason is that God has assured those who follow him that he will give them what they need. Jesus tells us not to worry (see Matthew 6:24-34).

The other reason is the availability of thousands of unfilled jobs — jobs for almost any skill you can name, jobs which are challenging and of crucial importance. These jobs are categorized by a rather old-fashioned term: missionary.

Man With a Mission

"Missionary" conjures up unpleasant images of 19th-century men in pith helmets swatting flies and preaching to naked savages. There are few, if any, such missionaries left. By the broadest definition of the word, a missionary is someone with a mission or purpose. Every Christian is a missionary in that sense, determined to obey God and to tell other people about Jesus. But "missionary" has acquired another definition over the years: someone with a mission *in another country or culture*. If you work out your mission in life as a Christian in another country, you are a missionary. You are likely to live in a modern city; you might be a teacher, offer technical assistance or help run a bookstore. The major difference between a missionary and a non-missionary is that a missionary lives outside the boundaries of his own country or culture.

No one should jump into that. The idea of living in a different culture or climate might seem exotic. You may win spiritual points among your friends for being a missionary. But those who go on such motives usually are shocked by a wearing, unpleasant discovery: "They're different from us."

Suppose you went to France as a missionary. France is more like America than most countries. But little things would irk you, even if you spoke perfectly fluent French. You would discover that there are no parks where you are allowed to walk on the grass — no open grassy spaces to throw a frisbee or lie in the sun. You would find that it is hard to make friends, because people are cautious and conservative. You might find that people talk endlessly about subjects that utterly bore you. You would find that people bathe less.

In some other culture you might find that people stand too close when they talk, arrive consistently late, never say "thank you," or tend to criticize others behind their backs. Being there can be lonely as well as frustrating, because it means leaving old friends and family behind. Even when you see them, they won't be able to visualize the life you're living.

Because of all these factors, it's hard to be effective in another culture. If you're afraid to tell your friends about your faith in Christ now, you can't expect that fear to disappear just because you got on a plane and flew to another culture. If you tend to become depressed easily, you can expect the same problem doubled in another culture.

You Are Needed

But there are some positive reasons why you ought to think about it. First, there are jobs. Translated, that means you are needed. Isn't it a healthier psychology to go to work where you are wanted, rather than to squeeze and fight your way into a job in America, knowing that almost anything you can do could be replaced with a want ad?

There is another reason, too: something Jesus said. Practically his last words before leaving earth were instructions to his hand-picked leaders, instructions

We'd sooner talk to an old friend than meet a new one. That is why Jesus' first word had to be "go."

passed on from generations of Christians to generations ever since. "Go," he said. "Go and make followers in every nation."

Human beings have an innate tendency to make themselves comfortable. We'd sooner talk to an old friend than meet a new one. That is why Jesus' first word had to be "go." Left to themselves, those first Christians wouldn't have taken news about Jesus beyond their home town. They might have been concerned about the people next door, but the unknown millions beyond the horizons? They couldn't imagine them.

Today TV and newspapers bring us into daily contact with outside cultures, but the expanded contact hasn't expanded our interest in leaving our comfort behin. Christianity, though it is worldwide, and stronger in some African and Asian countries than in America or Europe, has most of its "professionals" in America. Ninety per cent of the full-time Christian workers work with 10% of the world's population. There is a need for Christians to spread out. There is a need for Christians to obey Jesus' direction: "Go."

Not everyone should go. But more should. And I believe everyone should consider it. Want a job? ■

Urbana happens every three years.

Sponsored by Inter-Varsity Christian Fellowship, an organization that works with college students, Urbana is a gathering of 15,000 young people to talk about spreading Jesus outside America and Canada. Speakers, workshops and Bible studies direct themselves to hundreds of facets of that subject. Most Christian organizations which work overseas send representatives you can talk to about job openings. There's also music, multi-media and, if you're lucky, snow. It takes place on the University of Illinois campus December 26-31, and though it's primarily for college students, high-school seniors can attend. For information write Urbana, IVCF, 233 Langdon, Madison, Wisconsin 53703.

OPERATION JOB MATCH

If you're just out of high school, maybe you don't really know where you're going or what type of career you want. You want to serve God but you don't know what you want to do. Never fear. "Futures" exists especially for you, to pinpoint Christian service opportunities and, most important, show how to prepare for them.

Futures is a service of Intercristo, an organization based in Seattle that uses the computer to help bring people together — sort of like computer dating, but with a different goal in mind. Intercristo helps people eager to go into Christian work get together with organizations eager to have them.

As an applicant for Futures, you fill out a profile telling your background, interests, education, skills, all sorts of juicy information.* Send it along with a fee ($10 to help cover costs) and your data becomes computer food. After it's processed, you receive a list of job possibilities plus the amount of education needed, the language required, how the position is supported, the work experience necessary, opportunities for summer jobs and any other crucial information.

Intercristo isn't the final answer to your future in the working world. It has limitations and doesn't have the solution for everyone. But it can't hurt you to have your information run through the computer.

*Get applications and more information by writing to Intercristo, Box 9323, Seattle, Washington 98109, or call, toll free, 800-426-0507.

College

After high school, the next logical step for most graduates is college. There are other options to be sure, and this next section will point some of them out. But college is still the first big step for a lot of people.

What kind of college should you attend? How do you pick a college? How much should it cost? What do you do when you get there? These are a few of the questions we'll be looking at. You'll find out how to read a college catalog, who to ask for money, what to look for when visiting a campus . . . everything you need to know before you pack your toothbrush and tennies and trudge off to the ivory towers.

Neahl Klein

If the thought of sitting behind a desk four more years has got you seriously considering the French Foreign Legion, maybe it's time to look at a few more options. After all . . .

What's So Great About College?

■ College, college, college. By the time you are a senior in high school all you hear about is college. People come out of the woodwork to ask you which school you're going to. (Notice they never think to ask *if* you're going. College seems to be the logical conclusion to high school, like wet is to swimming. But there can be a lot better places to go after high school than college (there are worse places too, but we won't go into that).

Other Options

It is no secret anymore that the so-called "blue collar" worker can earn as much money as his college-educated "white-collar" counterpart. Often they earn more — plumbers, contractors, truckers, air-conditioning repairmen and brick layers are the Ph.D.'s of the working world. The only trick is to learn a skill that the world needs.

Each year colleges turn out thousands and thousands more skilled applicants than can ever get a job simply because there are more applicants than jobs. For example, in 1975, the Department of Labor estimated there would be approximately 4,300 new jobs for psychologists. Colleges turned out 58,400 B.A.'s in psychology — that left roughly 54,000 graduates who didn't get jobs (not as psychologists anyway).

Vocational schools can offer a much better job placement rate than a university. Fewer people go to vocational schools and there are far more job openings available for their graduates. There is a catch, however, and it's a dandy. You have to know exactly what it is you want to do before you start. It would be ridiculous to spend two years studying x-ray technology only to find out that you weren't even slightly interested in being an x-ray technician. A vocational school is not a job smorgasbord; it is no place to jump around sampling the menu. If (and it's a big if) you know yourself well enough, know what you would be happy doing for a number of years and have the all-consuming passion to devote to one interest, vocational school could be the best choice you could make.

Much the same could be said for apprenticeship. Apprenticeship is really only glorified "on-the-job training." You are paid a certain wage to learn a specific trade. Along the way varying degrees of competency must be mastered, there are tests that must be passed and sometimes licenses to be obtained. You receive top-quality training, both on-the-job and

by Steve Lawhead

Tim Stafford

classroom, a guaranteed salary from the first day and built-in increases along the way (regular union benefits, controlled working conditions, time-off, holidays, etc.)

With all that going for it, why don't more people choose apprenticeship instead of vocational school? Too much competition. It may take a carefully laid out campaign with no mistakes along the way to get into an apprenticeship program. Anyone interested in finding out more about apprenticeship should start at the State Employment Service Office nearby. For general information about apprenticeships write to: U.S. Department of Apprenticeship and Training, Department of Labor, Washington, D.C. 20202. Like vocational training, apprenticeship could be the best choice you could make after graduation if you meet the qualifications.

The Green Brigade

The military turns many people off. But now that the shooting has stopped and the draft is gone, the army is offering a pretty good deal. Both women and men are eligible for almost any program of the armed forces. The services offer 237 different occupational fields which they teach in on-the-job training at no cost — they even pay you while you're learning. And the pay isn't bad: $300 a month plus free living quarters, meals, clothing, medical and dental care, and social activities. Add all that up and it easily comes out to about $650 a month as a starting salary, respectable for any beginner in any field.

In addition to some of the best training available — training you can use when you return to civilian life — the armed forces also offer a tempting list of fringe benefits: travel opportunities; vacations — 30 days annually from the first year; opportunities to meet people; PX privileges — a 30 per cent discount on anything you'd ever want to buy; and more. Any recruiting officer can fill you in.

As an alternative to college, the army, navy, coast guard or marines can make you a good offer. But like anything else, check it out thoroughly — you're the only one who can decide what is right for you.

Who'll Volunteer?

Volunteer work is prestige work. Not the kind of prestige one usually thinks of in terms of money or fame, but in the eyes of the people volunteers help, there's no one respected more. It might mean helping younger kids in trouble with the law, elderly people, the disadvantaged or teaching a skill such as reading. Sometimes a little pay is offered to volunteers, sometimes not. Sometimes a volunteer position expands into a full-time paid occupation based on the skills you learn.

Social action groups are "in" now and offer a volunteer a chance to do something about the mess the world's in. Whatever your concern there is an organization which could use your help. The Peace Corps and Vista, which haven't been in the news lately, are still around looking for volunteers.

Volunteer work can provide the experience or skills needed to land you a job elsewhere when the time comes. It gives a taste of various fields such as social service, teaching, library work, environmental protection, museum work, politics or hospital administration without committing yourself to a lifelong career. You can find out more about the kind of volunteer work you'd enjoy by writing The National Center for Voluntary Action, 1735 I Street, NW, Washington, DC 20001. Or check with community organizations in your area; they are listed in the phone book.

College Reconsidered

If you've decided against college because you'd rather croak than sit another four years at a desk, or because you assume it's going to cost so much and you'd rather be making your fortune than spending it, maybe it's time to reconsider college as an option.

The truth is, the kind of jobs a high school kid can get on the open market leave an awful lot to be desired. They are usually dull, low paying and tedious. College can offer you a chance to get yourself together mentally and socially before you have to face the world. Many people get the mistaken idea, however, that going to college means you have to go four years full-time and pay for it all on the day you start. Not so.

Colleges are becoming more consumer-oriented every year. Most of them offer many kinds of programs — not just the four-year degree variety. Higher edu-

The kind of jobs a high school kid can get leave an awful lot to be desired. They are usually dull, low-paying and tedious. College can offer you a chance to get yourself together mentally and socially before you have to face the world.

cation in recent years has seen so many changes that college attendance can mean a hundred different things: from traveling abroad to thinking up your own courses and doing them yourself to receiving credit for something you already know. One, the University Without Walls, is an organization of 20 colleges offering students educational opportunities defined by students themselves — at work, home or in one or more schools.

Community colleges specialize in part-time, interest-oriented courses that students can take while holding down a part-time job.

There are so many ways to get a college degree nowadays that college itself provides an alternative to the traditional "college education." All it takes is a clear knowledge of what you want to do and motivation enough to find out who's offering the kind of program that seems to fit you. Here's a bit of information which could help you: colleges are no longer turning away qualified students due to overcrowding. In most places the reverse is true — private colleges desperately *need* students to stay in business. Let the college recruit *you*; make them give you the best deal they have. If you're not satisfied look elsewhere — it's a buyer's market.

Only you can tell if college is right or wrong for you. But if you find yourself asking questions about the world and where you fit in, college could help you find the answers. If you're not asking any questions, and you're planning on going to college because you can't think of anything better to do — maybe you'd better consider one of the alternatives mentioned here. *Alternatives to College* by Miriam Hecht and Lillian Traub is an excellent book for those wondering what to do with themselves after high school. But above all, talk to others — parents, friends, counselors — about your plans. Direct communication can often solve most of the problems of decision-making and help make whatever you do the best thing you ever did. ∎

There comes a time in your search for a college when you have to weigh all the arguments and information and decide which school you're going to. It's a lot easier if you begin by asking . . .

What Kind of School Do I Want?

■ Choosing a college is a little bit like getting married. There is a period of courtship when you are looking for a college and colleges are looking for you, an engagement after you have applied and been accepted, a short honeymoon after you arrive at college and before the first round of examinations and then the inevitable facing up to the realities of life together. If successful, the relationship will last for the rest of your life; you will always be known as an alumnus of your college.

And, as with getting married, there are the right and the wrong reasons for choosing a college. For instance, what difference does it *really* make that your brother or sister or best friend went (or is going) to a particular college? Or that this college has the best football team around? Or that it has 25,000 students?

Choosing a college, like marriage, demands serious thought and planning.

What Kind Of School Do You Want?

Before attempting to select, you should give some thought to what *kind* of school you want to attend. One of the most striking characteristics of American higher education today is its amazing diversity. You can choose from liberal arts colleges,

universities, community colleges, Bible colleges, Bible institutes or technical and vocational training schools.

The key question might be "What do you expect from college?" You may have definitely made up your mind about what type of work you want to do and will want to make sure your school has a strong program in your chosen area. But try to avoid the trip of too early specialization. If you are not absolutely sure what you want to do, it is especially important that you select a school with a balanced program that will give you the chance to sample different areas before specializing in any one.

Another vital consideration: how will it contribute to your spiritual growth? Groups of strong Christians can be found at many secular schools. There are many fine Christian schools today that are every bit as respectable academically as their secular neighbors . . . be sure you know the differences in purpose and function among Christian liberal arts colleges, Bible colleges and Bible institutes.

After you have done some thinking about these things on your own, talk them over with some of the people whose judgment you respect. Visit the counseling office in your high school and get

by Dr. C. Dorr Demaray,
Former President, Seattle Pacific College

Bob Combs

acquainted with your counselor and the materials he has available to you. Make an appointment with your pastor or youth leader. By all means involve your parents in all phases of the decision-making process.

Selecting The One You Want

When you feel you have pretty well decided what *kind* of school you want to attend, send for information from at least three schools of the same basic type. Do not be overly impressed by full-color brochures and glamorous photography. Compare the materials carefully, looking not only for the strengths emphasized by each, but also the hidden weaknesses either not mentioned or else glossed over with vague generalities. Look not only for breadth of offerings, but also for depth. Gauge the strength of the faculty not only by the number of full-time teachers in relation to the size of the student body, but also by the percentage who have earned advanced degrees — preferably at some other institution. Examine the extracurricular activities available — are they entirely inward-directed or are some aimed at expanding your awareness of the outside world with its problems and opportunities?

College

A lot goes into choosing the right school.
Be sure you know all your options.

David S. Strickler

What About Cost?

Involved in any decision about higher education today — unfortunately, but inevitably — is the consideration of cost. Your first choice should be the college which will provide the most appropriate education for your particular needs. Most colleges have extensive financial aid programs for those who would otherwise be unable to meet the full cost of a college education. It is not unusual for 40 per cent of a student body to be receiving some form of aid.

Do not rule out your first choice until you have explored all the possibilities of financial aid open to you. If you are admissible and have financial need, chances are very good that you will be eligible for some kind of help. A frank discussion among you, your parents and an admissions officer should result in a program designed to meet your full need. (If distance is a factor, this can be done by mail.) Such a program will typically consist of any one or a combination of grants, loans and guaranteed jobs on campus.

When To Begin

It's never too early to begin thinking about where you want to go to college. If you are freshly graduated and would like to attend college this fall but have not yet applied, time is running short. Most schools will still accept applications for admission, but many of them may have already allocated their available financial aid funds for the coming year. So act soon. ■

Unless you're a member of the monied elite,
any talk about college is also a discussion of money.
You need to know . . .

How Much Will It Cost?_____

■ Trying to figure how much it costs to go to college is a little like buying a car. The ads say the cost is only $3,289. That is, $3,289 *plus* tax and license. Then there are the dealer's preparation charges and shipping costs. On top of that, if you want tinted glass, steel-belted tires, automatic transmission, radio or anything else — that's extra. Your $3,289 economy car ends up costing $4,000 or more.

The cost of college is like that. There are extra costs that aren't always readily visible. To get a true picture of how big a bite it's going to take out of your finances, you have to find out those extra costs and add them up.

The basic charge at any college is tuition. It is figured in little lumps called credit hours, and many colleges charge a flat rate for each credit hour taken. Others simply charge a blanket rate that covers everything from 12 to 18 hours of credit taken each semester. Sometimes there is a difference in price between full-time and part-time credit hours. Usually, a full-time student is one who takes from 12 to 18 hours of classes per semester. A part-time student takes from 2 to 12 hours (each class is loosely considered as consisting of 3 to 5 credit hours). Most four-year colleges require at least 120 semester credit hours for graduation and a bachelor's degree.

The Highs and Lows

Tuition costs vary greatly from college to college. For example, the University of Illinois charges $660 for tuition per year — that's pretty low. Wagner College in New York charges $2,600 — that's getting up there, but some private colleges are higher. On the whole, Christian colleges and all private colleges are higher than state institutions; Bible colleges are less than either. But tuition isn't the only charge you'll be paying at school. There are the costs of room and board and fees to figure in.

The cost of room and board varies also. It will be higher in an area where living expenses are higher, such as around metropolitan areas. On the average, you can expect to pay about $1,150 per year for room and board. But that doesn't include all those miscellaneous extras such as snacks, movies, dates, games and any number of other "necessities." Shaving cream, make-up, laundry, soap and toothpaste also fall under this heading. Be sure to add those into your total.

Fees are what the college charges for handling you, among other things. The

by Steve Lawhead

David S. Strickler

College

cost of maintaining your administrative paperwork is sometimes figured in here. Sometimes a little of this fee money is turned over to the student activities committee for use in bringing speakers and musical groups to the campus, for homecoming festivities and other student-centered activities.

Glancing through a catalog will clue you in to what some of those "extras" include. For example: residence hall social fee, $75; late registration fee, $10; physical education deposit, $5; automobile registration fee, $1; parking sticker, $5; lab fees, $15; transcripts, $1 each; course credit by examination fee, $20. Each college has its own list.

If you are living away from home, don't forget to add the cost of travel to and from college at least twice a year — you'll probably return home for the winter and spring vacation. Add to that a one-way ticket when you leave for college in the fall, and another for when you return in the summer.

Books! You can't go to school without them, and every year they cost more and more. Most colleges have bookstores that will buy back some of the books at a pro-rated allowance after you're done with them, and you can usually buy used books there as well. That helps. Upperclassmen are a good source of cheap, used books. But you'll have to hunt them up on your own. Still, it's going to be anywhere from $150 to $200 per year for books. It's not uncommon to find a bill of $50 for books for one course!

If you are going to take any classes in art, photography or other special interest areas, then art supplies, paper, film, etc., can easily bring the bookstore tab to $200.

The last thing to add in is pocket money, that extra-extra money everyone needs just to get along. Assume $10 a week will get you by, and that's low. You can easily spend that much on coffee alone during test week!

That should just about take care of all the extras. So, how much does it cost to go to college? Here are three comparative price lists:

Costs Per Year

	Low	Middle	High
Tuition	$ 660	$1,300	$2,900
Room & Board	$ 600	$1,150	$1,550
Fees	$ 25	$ 150	$ 375
Travel	$ 0	$ 185	$ 300
Books	$ 90	$ 200	$ 250
Personal	$ 175	$ 330	$ 550
Total	$1,550	$3,315	$5,925

Here's Help

Now that you know how much it's going to cost, you're wondering how you're going to pay for it. Your dear old Uncle Sam can help. Through the Bureau of Higher Education the federal govermment offers four main programs for financial aid to students.

1) National Defense Loans allow students to borrow up to $1,000 per academic year, to a combined total of $5,000. Repayment and interest begin

nine months after completing school. With 10 years to repay the loan, the annual percentage rate of interest is three per cent on the unpaid balance. You can get 50% of the loan forgiven by teaching for five years. Teachers of handicapped or low-income children and those who, after graduation, enter the armed forces get even better repayment terms.

2) Educational Opportunity Grants

Don't panic when you add up the total — your dear old Uncle Sam can help with financial aid programs set up especially for you

provide $200 to $1,000 per academic year and need not be repaid. The college matches the E.O.G. money and determines eligibility on the basis of financial need rather than academic achievement.

3) College Work-Study programs allow students to attend classes full time while working 15 hours per week during the school year. Pay ranges from the current minimum wage to $3.50 an hour at either on-campus or off-campus jobs.

4) Guaranteed Loans for College and Vocational Students allow a student to borrow from local lending institutions up to $1,500 per academic year to a combined total of $7,500. Repayment begins nine to 12 months after graduation, usually lasting five to 10 years. Seven percent is the maximum interest rate which can be charged. Many participating banks require at least a six-month depositor status of the student or his parents.

For more information on any of these programs, write: Division of Student Financial Aid, Bureau of Higher Education, U.S. Office of Education, Washington, D.C. 20202. Also, contact the director of student financial aid at the college you wish to attend.

Other government agencies direct financial-aid programs to special groups of students: Veterans Administration (for veterans and children of certain vets), U.S. Public Health Service (students in nursing, medicine and other health professions), Bureau of Mines (a work-study program) and Office of Water Resources Research (also a work-study program). Each state has an office of higher education, providing information on guaranteed student loans.

A handy publication to obtain is *Financial Aid for Higher Education*. Send one dollar to the Superintendent of Documents, Washington, D.C. 20402, requesting the booklet (Order No. FS 5.255.55056). It lists colleges and universities participating in federal financial-aid programs and provides other financial-aid information. ■

Colleges are run by their catalogs. Everything you need to know is in there — all you have to do is decipher it . . .

How Do I Read a College Catalog?

■ When I began shopping for a college, I made two mistakes. First, I didn't know what a good college was, so I didn't know what to look for. Second, I assumed the educational world was totally reliable in all its advertising. If a school claimed to be great, it must be great, I thought. I didn't know then that, while most advertising *is* honest and genuinely helpful, the name of the advertising game is "accentuate-the-good-points."

The first step in avoiding these mistakes is a careful study of the school catalog, a paperback book put out by the school to inform, enlighten and, they hope, impress you. I attended a total of eight different institutions of higher learning before I pushed out into the wide world. In the process, I read a lot of college catalogs.

Whether reading it in the library or receiving it through the mail, you should open a catalog realizing there are some topics on which the book is absolutely trust-worthy:

1. Money

The catalog will tell you how much each course will cost, the expense of living in the dormitories, fees and scholarships available. It may offer a helpful round figure to estimate your expenses per year. Usually such a figure is slightly on the low side.

2. Course requirements

The catalog will list courses available and required for various fields. Many schools have a large number of courses required for everyone, regardless of their major field. You should notice the language requirements: many schools require two years of a foreign language other than the one you studied in high school. Be alert to extra off-campus requirements such as a summer or semester spent on a special project. This might add to your college experience, but you should be the one to decide if you can afford it.

3. Physical facts of the campus.

The catalog will usually list the number and kinds of buildings, acres of campus, number of books in the library, number of students and faculty, etc. (One insight to the contrary, though: what you see may not be what you get. Some catalogs might show several attractive students gathered around a sophisticated microscope in a bright, shiny, stainless steel, chemistry laboratory. When you arrive there, you might

by Steve Board

LITTLEWIT COLLEGE

Credibility Gap, North Carolina 77174

OFFICIAL COURSE DESCRIPTIONS

110 ASTRONOMY

A survey of the major celestial objects — planets, stars, 747's and big, floating space things; a study of their characteristics and behavior in the universe. Students will learn basic astronomy methods, such as how to distinguish a planet from a galaxy, the difference between an asteroid and a telescope, and how to make everyone think you've really seen a U.F.O. All students will write a term paper on the subject — "Alien Life in the Universe: Where Do They Come From? What Do They Want? And Why Do They Like Elton John?"

3 hrs credit

388 FOUNDATIONS OF ABSTRACT ALGEBRA

Vector spaces, polynomials, topological composition, eigenvalues, elementary number theory are discussed. Development of mathematical concepts are traced from early Egyptian number painting to the invention of the zero in North Dakota. Final test requires that students demonstrate how to count, add columns and pronounce astronomically large numbers correctly (see astronomy 110). Prerequisite: 2 yrs high school algebra or 3 yrs "Sesame Street."

3 hrs credit

311 INDEPENDENT STUDY IN BIOCHEMISTRY

This course offers two practical options: 1) the theoretical study of a particular topic in biochemistry, or 2) cleaning up the laboratory and looking after the white mice. Student initiative and progress are considered as basis for final credit. The approval of department head is required. (Mops and pails can be obtained from maintenance dept.; feeding schedules for the mice are posted near the cages.)
credit: TBA

418 AVIAN BIOLOGY (Urban)

Ornithological study of various species of common city birds. Class work related to field experience as students discover how to spot birds in large metropolitan areas. Techniques of identification and taxonomy explored. Topics covered: Pigeon Populations in U.S. and Abroad (And Why There Are So Many); Puzzling Pigeon Facts; Pigeon Husbandry.

3 hrs credit

257 PRACTICUM IN PIANO PEDAGOGY

Focus on preparing student to give instruction to and evaluate performances by amateurish piano students, develop techniques for winding the metronome and watch films of people playing the piano incorrectly. Prerequisite: 2 major piano concertos, 5 hit songs or 1 Elton John concert.

1 hr credit

103

OFFICIAL COURSE DESCRIPTIONS

499c ORGANIZED CRIME (workshop)
A short history of organized crime in the U.S. will be presented with emphasis on its relationship to contemporary institutions. Also, an examination of the influence of crime on the moral values of criminals. Students will be divided into small groups for workshop experience in racketeering, bootlegging, numbers running and bribing public officials. Each student will present to the class a summary report on a personal project. Pick one: bank robbery, extortion, tax evasion, kidnapping. There will be one field trip — 6 weeks in Joliet State Prison. Prerequisite: viewing *Godfather (parts I & II)* (understanding Marlon Brando's speaking parts).
5 hrs credit

346 PHILOSOPHY — KNOWLEDGE AND REALITY
Systems of thought on the reality of knowledge and the reality of reality, as well as the more basic knowledge of knowledge are examined. Students are taught the fundamental practices of determining whether something is real and are encouraged to find out if they know anything. Readings in the works of major philosophers are inspected for resemblances of Plato, Oristhenes, Heidegger, Bunker and John (Elton) are reviewed. Prerequisite: Abnormal Psychology 210.
3 hrs credit

111 SURVEY OF GREAT AMERICAN POETRY — POE TO McKUEN
Great American poets studied. Analysis of the poem as wall decoration and big money-maker considered. Students will manufacture their own synthetic poems after the manner of McKuen. (Negotiating a publishing and recording contract may be covered if time permits.) Jack Frost's great poem, "Stopping by Woods on a Smoggy Evening,"; Carl Sandpile's homage to an eternal city, "Muncie"; Poe's classics, "The Trained Crow" and "Colorado" are critiqued.
3 hrs credit

323 ARGUMENTATION AND DEBATE
Group discussion as an effective method of problem-solving. Attention moves progressively from the study of argumentation, analysis and discussion of issues, to name-calling, harassment, boycotting and brawling. Students asked to build repertoire of argumentation techniques, including: hurt, disgust, temper tantrums, nervous fits, pitiful crying and righteous indignation. Topics of interest form basis of reports by class members. Examples: How to Win an Argument You Didn't Start; Kung Fu As a Persuasive Technique; Kissing and Making Up: The Joy of Compromise. Required text: *How to Be Your Own Best Friend*.

—Steve Lawhead

4 hrs credit

discover that it's the only micro-scope they own, and they took the picture in the school kitchen!)

4. Accreditation

Colleges and universities are subject to independent grading agencies that evaluate them as educational facilities. This is the nearest to a *Consumers' Report* we have on colleges. The accreditors examine a school's facilities, faculty qualifications, curriculum, records of graduates and financial resources (they frown on colleges that go bankrupt in the middle of the school year!). The school gets either a pass or a fail. *You should know that some schools that fail the test are as good as some that pass.* A Bible institute, for instance, may not even desire accreditation as a liberal arts school. But you should also know that a non-accredited school may give you problems in the future when you apply to a graduate school (post-college study). If you are going into pre-med, for example, avoid any school that is not accredited.

Be alert in determining accreditation. Some schools will publish that they are licensed by the state, approved for veterans and other official-sounding terms. This is not the same as regional accreditation. Look for one of the six regional associations (New England, Middle States, Southern, North Central, Western or Northwest) if you're interested in using your education as a step-ping stone to graduate school or certain occupations.

* * *

With that, we get into areas about which a catalog can be unreliable.

1. No catalog can completely describe the extent of Christian commitment on campus.

After all, the book is prepared by the college, and they are not about to say the place is a spiritual wasteland, even if it is. Furthermore, there is no way to measure piety and devotion to God. The one thing that can be measured is the degree of required "religious" activity — chapel attendance, avoidance of certain activities such as dancing and attending movies, participation in some Christian work like Sunday school teaching, etc. The catalog probably will state these requirements clearly — though perhaps in a small type on an obscure page. Decide if these guidelines are what you're willing to live with.

2. No school can legitimately claim it will get you into any graduate school program (such as medical school or law school) or that it will get you a job.

I saw a piece of advertising from a small institution, boasting that one of its recent graduates had been accepted at Columbia University for work on a master's degree. The impression was that this student was typical of their graduates — they could get into major university. Actually, as I found out later, the student in question had come close to bribing Columbia to accept his bachelor's degree; they had never heard of the student's school and were reluctant to consider his application. Moral: if you have long-range career plans that involve further study after your first college degree, ask the graduate schools about the college in question. Find out how easy it will be to get accepted.

3. The college catalog is not the best source for a description of its academic, intellectual and social atmosphere.

The school can claim to stimulate relevant, intellectual and personal interaction, train The Whole Man and have air-conditioned classrooms. But the only thing you can check on is the air conditioning. The other claims are a matter of opinion. A visit to the campus may tell

you how stimulating or intellectual the school is. Sit in on some classes and, above all, visit the campus bookstore. The bookstore will tell you what people there are reading. If it stocks only sweat-shirts, mugs and required textbooks, the campus may not be the super-relevant intellectual place it claims to be.

* * *

Now a word on some areas you will have to make up your own mind about.

1. The faculty.

The catalog will list the faculty with their academic degrees. Almost all of them will have master's degrees, and a good many should have doctorates (Ph.D's). Beware of a list padded with so-called honorary doctoral degrees, such as D.D. Sometimes colleges and univer-

David S. Strickler

The time when you're standing in line to pull class cards is not the time to be thumbing through your catalog — to get the most out of it, you need to take time to study it.

sities give a prominent figure a doctor's degree as a way of saying "thank you" for some great contribution. This honorary degree is not the same as the degree earned only after years of study. For example, the vice-presidency of one small religious school is filled by a "Dr. John Smith" (not his real name). What is left untold is that he was given the "Dr." in recognition of his organizing ability for church busing programs. Not so academic.

While you are looking at the list of faculty, notice where they studied. If they all came from one school, it may be a bad sign. Small colleges can suffer from this. As a general principle, the faculty of a college should come from many graduate schools, so there can be a stimulating variety of opinion on campus. Without this, the school may be ingrown and heavy on a "party line" (that is, a few ideas it stresses in an unbalanced way). But you must make up your own mind about the school's faculty. A small faculty is usually a sign of friendly, personal interaction to come.

2. What the school really prepares you for.

If you plan to major in English or history, does the school seem to have a strong English or history department? Does it offer a variety of courses in your major? What do the graduate schools in your field think of the school you are considering? If you plan to study in a theological seminary, for example, you should be aware that some seminaries do not recommend a Bible college for the bachelor's degree, preferring instead a broad liberal arts education. That doesn't make Bible colleges or institutes inferior. The point is that you should know what the school of your choice will prepare you for and what fields of graduate study it is not well suited for.

3. Finally, you must make up your own mind on one of the common dilemmas facing a Christian student: should you attend a Christian college or a secular school, such as a state university?

The arguments on both sides are long and inconclusive. God's will for you may be either one, and you should remain open to either possibility. If God leads you to a secular campus, several organizations of Christian students probably exist there. A letter to their headquarters will connect you with their staff at the university you mention.* Christian students can be looking for you when you get there.

The catalog is a limited tool in selecting a college or university. It tells you a few important facts about the school. But it should be read critically and balanced with a wide range of opinions from people who know colleges. And reading in that critical fashion is a good way to get started on higher education. ■

*Some Christian student organizations: Inter-Varsity Christian Fellowship, 233 Langdon St., Madison, Wisconsin 53703
Campus Crusade for Christ, Arrowhead Springs, San Bernardino, California 92404
The Navigators, Colorado Springs, Colorado 80901
Inter-Varsity Christian Fellowship of Canada, 745 Mt. Pleasant Rd., Toronto 298, Ontario.

A college catalog can only take you so far, then you have to make up your mind. But before you do . . .

Why Not Take the Grand Tour?

by Stephen Erickson

■ It's all over. No more long, complicated forms to fill out. No more trying to remember your mother's maiden name or the last time you were sick enough to go to the doctor. No more attempts to cram your entire autobiography onto a half page. The college applications are all behind you. Now there's only the waiting and waiting and waiting.

Every day anticipation becomes worse. You almost attack the mailman to get what's in his bag, only to find bills for your parents and a supermarket flyer. You shake out the pages of the flyer to make sure nothing's hidden. Nothing is.

Finally you get an answer. Not one reply but three — all form letters beginning, "We are pleased to inform you that you have been accepted for the academic year of . . ."

You weren't even sure you would make it into one college, but now three are eagerly awaiting your arrival! You have to choose one but the catalogs all look alike. Now what? A sophisticated game of eenie-meenie-minie-mo?

There's only one thing left to do. Set your priorities firmly in mind and go visiting. Drop in on the colleges in question to find out what the catalogs can't tell

you.* By the process of elimination you should end up with one college (but if you're really picky you might end up with none at all).

So when's the best time of year to set out on a college spy mission? The bad times are whenever anything special is going on at the college, things like Homecoming, Parents' Day or Founder's Day. At these times the college puts on a "special face" and glosses over cracks in the veneer to impress alumni and other potential donors. The college is jammed with non-college people, all sporting name tags and wandering around campus like it's a county fair.

The Grand March

Many colleges sponsor special "high school weekends," when teens can supposedly see what college is *really* like. They're a riot, but fun may be all you'll get — not a clear picture of the college scene.

On "high school weekends" hundreds of your peers will share the two-day college experience with you. Not only does

*It's a good idea to visit colleges before you get acceptance notices. When you send in your applications is a good time to start planning a visit.

College _____

it make you feel as if you never left your high school, but the mass invasion puts the college students on edge. In turn, the snubbed high schoolers either try to act like college students, or melt into giddiness.

Another drawback to the "high school weekend" is that every minute is planned for you. Dinner at 5:00. Orientation at 6:30. Name Tag Carnival at 9:00. "This Is a Dormitory" at 10:00. This leaves little time for serious, below-the-surface investigation.

It's safe to say that the best time to visit a college is when nothing special is happening. Try to pick an "ordinary day in the life." Be sure to include a Friday or Monday so you can check out some classes.

Once you've decided on a time, let the office of admissions (registrar) know you're coming and for what reason. They'll arrange all the essentials.

First is the Grand March or (as it is more commonly known) the guided tour of the campus. Your guide, who was chosen for his smileability and eagerness to earn a few extra bucks, will help familiarize you with the college. He'll point out things like how much bronze was needed to make the statue of the college's founder and how the pigeons have been a problem all year. He'll whisk you through corridors as if you were making a comparative study of hallways. And he'll give you a quick lesson on campus architecture.

The Grand March is fast and furious, giving you little more than a personal version of catalog trivia, unless you really probe and your guide doesn't mind having his brain picked. It does give a good knowledge of campus geography.

If you're staying more than one day you will most likely be billeted in a dorm with a college freshman. Usually your host or hostess will be friendly and answer all of your questions about dorm life and which professors to avoid, introduce you to other students, take you to some of his classes and keep you warm and dry under his wing.

Check It Out

But even if you're left entirely on your own, you can manage solo. Remember those priorities? What you're looking for in a college? Make the most of your solitude and anonymity. Nose about a little.

Check out the facilities for starters. For example, if chemistry is one of your main academic pursuits, you had better investigate the labs.

Intramural sports? Find out why the practice field looks like a horticulturist's lawn. Maybe the grass is nice because no one is allowed to play on it. The track that you thought was hard-packed mud and cinders — upon closer inspection it could prove to be a professional rubberized material. The nets on the tennis courts may be down because brand-new ones are going up. By snooping a little you can find out many things that the catalog could never tell you.

Be sure to browse in the library. Pick a subject you know something about and see what books they have on it. If you flip through a dust-encrusted book and the pages crumble into brown flakes, it's a good sign the library isn't up to par.

Most college dining halls are a far cry from Dearest Mother, but it's a wonder what some cafeteria chefs can do. Others got their training in the Army. To discover what kind of cook the college has . . . eat.

If you have to cut your mashed potatoes with a knife and the gravy slides down your throat in one gelatinous strand,

Make the most of your solitude and anonymity, find out what the college is really like

think twice. Ask yourself, is academic excellence really worth malnutrition?

Once you have surveyed the physicals, move on to phase two — attend some classes, not just one, but a good cross section, preferably three or more. You should choose at least one required course and then fill in with courses that interest you or that you anticipate taking. And if you're really brave, sit in on an upper-division course.

Class Action

You'll find some college classes are not that different from your classes at high school. In fact, the whole atmosphere may be similar. Students lay sprawled over their desks in an experimental learn-while-you-sleep program. The try-to-be-hip professor with the sprayed hair and too-short bell-bottoms accents his lecture with vernacular like "keen," "neato" and "spiffy."

Then again it could be a stimulating lecture with a lot of give and take. If it is, and there are some questions you want answered from a faculty viewpoint, try to get an appointment with the professor. If he's not booked up, he'll talk to you and give you his perspectives on the institution.

That leaves you with one more perspective to get — the students'. You've probably been getting this all along, but a little in-depth exposure wouldn't hurt.

You'll get more of the actual flavor of the college from the students than from any other source. Where's a good place to listen? It's hard to say. Certainly not outside the dean's office. Anywhere students congregate and are relatively candid will do. The student union (the entertainment capital on campus) is one suggestion. Dorm rooms and lounges are another.

Chances are good you will have to be satisfied with a normal bull session or nothing at all. If you work up enough gall to join in a bull session, you'll have to listen with discernment. Grab the gold and sift away the sludge. With this done, sit back and relax until your visit comes to an end. If things go right you should return home with enough data to make an intelligent choice. Then again, there's always eenie, meenie, minie . . . ∎

Once you sign your name on the dotted line, college has you in its grip. You're in a race with every other first-time college student, and the outcome is in doubt. You wonder . . .

Will I Survive My Freshman Year?

by Lois Breiner

■ If you're college-bound next fall, you've probably been getting volumes of advice on life within the hallowed halls. However, if high school guidance counselors advise you to forget foreign languages, you may discover your favorite subject is Swahili. Girls who hear lurid stories from upperclassmen about every guy on campus being after their bodies often find themselves with dozens of platonic male companions ("I love you — like a sister"). People try to tell you that college students care about their clothes. So you spend $599.95 on a new "college look" wardrobe with all the shades of Ivy League only to discover that everyone on campus is decked out in denim and burlap.

Mainly, first-year survival requires a good attitude and a good sense of humor. As you arrive on campus with a nervous stomach, 920 pounds of luggage and the bugged-eye look that belongs exclusively to bewildered freshmen, be prepared for some surprises. To soften the culture shock, we've talked to freshmen who *did* survive (some just barely) and have come up with the true dope on what to expect.

Life on the Tundra

Freshman year: you're like a pioneer crossing the great, unspoiled tundra of your life. Your first year on the tundra teaches you a lot about yourself. For instance, you will discover that there is nothing you can't put up with at one time or another. Whether it's the cafeteria's weekly serving of Mystery Meat, the irrelevant core courses that have nothing to do with your major (zoology for a voice major?) or your roommate's snort-wheeze snoring (dorm life is a great preparation for marriage), you'll soon learn to compromise, ignore it or live with it.

One of the early rigors is freshman orientation. This consists of helpful sessions which give out invaluable facts like the year the college was founded and where you can locate the gravesite of the first college president's dog.

Despite orientation, freshman year can be your Age of Enlightenment. Not only are you introduced to great nuggets of knowledge, but you also learn how to do your laundry. You take part in tests of sheer physical strength, such as carrying 35 library books up nine flights of stairs when none of the elevators are working. You come to grips with your intestinal fortitude as you face the fragrance of a fetal pig marinated in formaldehyde for your 7 a.m. biology lab.

Roommate Rifts

One problem that can erupt is the roommate hassle. Chances are you've

College

Welcome to the

MONKEY HOUSE
Guide to College Freshmen

■ Noted scholar and educator Fletchwood Bumbelfungus, in an exclusive interview with CAMPUS LIFE Magazine, answers the questions most asked by entering college freshmen about college life.

Q **I've never been away from home before. Will I get homesick?**

A There's a good chance you won't. Our government is currently readying enough serum to vaccinate every college freshman against the dreaded *domecilia* virus that causes homesickness. You may, however, come down with any number of other things, including swine fever, tetanus typhoid, black plague or athlete's foot.

Q **What is a Dean and what does it do?**

had your own bedroom at home, a shrine entered only by a privileged few. If not, at least you and your siblings have lived together long enough for them to know you'll beat on them if they play Chicago or the Stones while you're trying to study. But your college roommate doesn't know that. Your roommate must be educated.

Your college probably will not offer luxurious quarters to incoming freshmen. Usually at least two of you will be crammed into a room which seems about five feet by five feet. However, small can become smaller when your roommate plants a life-sized teddy bear in the middle of the room ("I've had Melvie since I was 5. Hasn't he held up well?") and a 25-can supply of pop on top of *your* closet ("It's right next to the window where it'll keep cold.").

To cut down on roommate rifts — and life is much easier if they're kept to a minimum — a bit of common sense, courtesy and respect for each other goes a long way. You'll find roommates are handy critters to have around. During your first week they're great people to sit with at meals. An unwritten loyalty develops between roommates. When you get sick, they're always on hand to bring you food and add a word of cheer (it helps to make up for all the open windows you had to sleep under when the temperature was .zero). Roommates are nice to have around at 3 a.m. after you've broken up with your girl friend or boyfriend and need someone to talk to. Roommates should be willing to put themselves out just a little bit to help each other. The resulting friendship is worth the extra trouble.

The Fate of the Too-free Spirits

Most colleges offer a big taste of freedom. Nobody breathes over your shoulder and prods you to do your work. You don't have to go to class, you don't have to do your assignments, but you also don't have to come back to college after your first semester. Remember the slogan: It's not funky to be a flunkie. A lot of kids can't hack the freedom — they don't know what to do with it or how to use it to their advantage.

Consider the case of Gregarious Gertrude. Gert went to the University of Moosiana (Moo U) with the noble intent of earning a degree. However, during the first week she started falling behind in her work, a critical state since she was attending only orientation lectures. Her pattern continued into her classes. Gert was easily sidetracked at night or during the day or whenever it was time for her to study. Something of greater priority always leaped up. Like a long overdue letter to her second cousin Ernie, or a deep, soul-scratching discussion about the value of hair spray or an emergency consolation of a depressed zoo major whose gerbil died.

Whenever there was a party or bull session or informal gethering or superficial

A Every college has a person named Dean whom everyone is allowed to call by his first name. It is his job to make sure the students maintain the academic standards of the school — that is, to talk quietly in the halls and to keep their desks in straight lines.

Q What is it like living in a dorm?

A It is like living with a band of Hungarian gypsies in a telephone booth. It is like trying to maintain a meaningful relationship with a troop of hostile baboons. It is like having 137 mothers. It is like being trapped in a root cellar with Gomer Pyle. It is like spending the night with the Waltons (every night).

Q What are my chances of getting through college without borrowing money?

A 68,000:1.

College

Q What is there in the way of entertainment at college?

A Late night studying for a test, lack of spending money, grouchy roommates and parents who constantly worry what you're up to. These are just a few of the things that stand in the way of entertainment at college.

Q What's the best way to study for exams?

A One of the easiest and most popular ways to study is a relatively new theory called Information Absorption by Osmosis. The idea is that the close proximity of books is beneficial; hence, prolonged exposure to the written word is desirable. A tour through any college library provides ample demonstration of this method; you'll see hardworking students facedown, sound asleep on their books.

Q Can I waive classes which do not apply to me or are repetitive?

meeting of the minds, Gert was there. Her lissome life-style soon waned as she arrived at mid-term 29,568 pages behind in her reading. She soon learned there is no easy solution for survival when one slides into this mess.

Gert figured she could a) cram, b), take an incomplete in every subject, c) get sick, d) bluff her way through her exams, e) none of the above. She opted for "d," and as a result, that letter spelled out her mid-semester average.

Gertrude's story is true. She miraculously survived her freshmen year, as well as three years following. But her grades never improved . . . much. Her "study habits" had been formulated during the first week and never changed in four years.

It's strange what freedom can do to a person. No matter how permissive your parents may have been, it's different when they are not around. At college, you have no one to account to, and how you deal with your new freedom is entirely up to you. You'll discover there was a certain security in living with your parents. It may have been annoying to you to have them lecturing, ordering or nagging, but it did eliminate the trials of having to make difficult personal choices. Now *your* decisions settle what's right for you.

You can't help but notice classroom life is a little tougher as a freshman. Especially when your literature class is supposed to read *Moby Dick* in two days. It's up to you just how much time and effort you put into your work.

College Lets You "Know Thyself"

Freshman year gives you a chance to start a whole new life for yourself. The people you meet have no preconceived notions of who you are or were. You're no longer filed into high school categories of "brain-child," "super-jock" or "yucky-creep." It's hard at first because there is no clique of old friends around to offer reassurance that what you are doing is right.

You'll find there is freedom to develop and express yourself in new ways. You can be whoever you want to be: you can retreat inside yourself or become aggressive and outgoing. You can dye your hair, grow a beard, shave your head (the last two only if you're a guy). The first few months you're apprehensive as to how people will treat you. Will they accept you? Will you make good friends like you had in high school? Just remember that everyone around you is groping and looking for acceptance also. Chances are the friends you make in college will be closer to you than your friends from high school. College lets you get to know people in a deeper, more mature way, and the resulting relationships are more lasting. But it doesn't happen overnight.

"Everybody's-a-genius-but-me"

At first you'll notice that everybody in all your college classes is smarter than you. They've all read *War and Peace* (and

A Yes, you can. This is sometimes very tricky. Most students simply prefer to wave to professors, friends or casual acquaintances.

Q What's a good way to choose a college?

A Get together with 10 other friends. Form a circle and everyone pick a number. The number closest to 27 starts by shouting out, "I'll take Vassar!" Continue until everyone has picked a college. Anyone who can't think of a college loses his turn and must take whatever's left over.

Q I was president of my senior class in high school. Could I become president in college?

A It isn't likely. In view of the tremendous expenditure of time and money involved in the promotion of a presidential campaign, most college students just can't hack it. And although many past presidents were college graduates, the American public

College

has never yet voted a student into the White House.

Q Many students get married in college. Is it easy to find a husband?

A Yes. There are many husbands in college, but most girls prefer to marry *single* men instead. That narrows the field considerably.

Q Is the food at college as bad as they say it is?

A Of course not — it's worse. At most colleges the food is so bad students are required to sign a written affidavit swearing never to reveal the true nature of the food they eat. All students have to sign if they wish to eat and/or graduate. (Ask the head honcho of the cafeteria how much he pays in malpractice insurance.)

Wheaton College

Making popcorn in the bathroom is something your mother never taught you — you'll learn a lot of things when you go away to college.

Q What is this new pass/fail grading system some colleges have now?

A There is really nothing new about this system, which was popular during the Dark Ages. Classrooms then were presided over by tyrannical headmasters who ran around yelling at the students, "You either pass this class, or you fail!" Nothing has changed.

Q What is the difference between GRE's and SAT's?

A GRE refers to tests you take if you want to go on to graduate school after college and SAT refers to traffic on the Santa Ana freeway, or those great big jets that go real fast and make a lot of noise — I forget which.

College

Q I've seen many bald men graduate from college. This leads me to wonder, if I graduate from college, will I lose my hair?

A Findings from current studies are inconclusive. In one experiment, eight rhesus monkeys were enrolled at Yale University, and four others took jobs at a factory in Trenton, New Jersey. Of the eight Yale monkeys, only three graduated. Of the three, two were bald and the other remained normal (although it did change its hair color as a sophomore). Of the working monkeys, one was laid off and two others were promoted to plant foreman. The monkey remaining on the assembly line developed severe baldness; the rest showed no signs of losing their

liked and/or understood it), *Beowolf* in the original Olde English, and they work crossword puzzles in Latin for fun. And there you sit with your backlog of movie and TV trivia festering in your mind cavities. Don't worry — you'll be surprised at how much you've learned after a few classes — or at least how much you discover you know. It's natural to intimidate yourself at first and put yourself down as the freshman vegetable.

College classes make you aware that learning for its own sake can be exciting and sometimes challenging. There's a great chance for growth and research on the college level. Some professors are brilliant and you'll look forward to their lectures. Most of them are usually genial about talking after class. They like to get to know you and will gladly help you if you're having trouble.

Beware the College Staff of Life: Pizza and Other Goodies

Pizza is an essential element for surviving your freshman year. It serves as a substantial substitute when the cafeteria has nothing more gourmet to offer than barbequed swordfish, oatmeal salad and rhubarb pudding. Other dietary supplements include cookies, popcorn, potato chips, pretzels, candy bars. You may find your creative instincts seem to flow only when triggered by Tootsie Pops, Oreos, Twinkies or any other plastic snack that turns on your taste buds. Without trying very hard, you can put on enough pounds to last you through graduate school. Extra goodies also have a way of eating up extra money, too, so be careful you don't put all your money where your mouth is.

Homesickitis

No matter how well things go for you, you'll still wake up some morning and find the whole world is dark with no chance of getting bright again. But hang on. No matter how impersonal and detached a school may seem, there are always people around to help you. Deans are willing to listen, and upperclassmen can throw in a word of advice — they know how it is; they've been there. And a call home does a lot for the morale at both ends of the line.

Rah, Rah College!

Perhaps at one time in your life, a parent, grandparent, uncle or cousin lifted you onto his or her knobby knee and told you that your college years would be the "best years of your life." Freshmen hear this phrase a lot during their first year — especially during orientation sessions. After a few weeks of college, however, you may find it hard to believe.

The people telling you this might be thinking of the Big Game or the Big Party after the Big Game, sort of the rah, rah, rah type of experience. But that stuff isn't nearly so important as the emotional and intellectual maturing which takes place in college. It happens. And it's all worth it. And you *will* survive. ■

hair. Thus, scientists concluded that college did affect hair loss. However, the findings were later invalidated when it was discovered that one of the monkeys who had been promoted was wearing a toupee.

Q What is the secret to staying interested in college?

A Girls/guys. Any upperclassman can tell you girls/guys make everything more interesting (depending, of course, upon which sex you are).

Q What does it mean when a course has a lab?

A It means you'll only be getting three hours of credit for an 18-hour class. ■

–by Steve Lawhead